SHADES
OF
GRAY

ANDY GRAY

SHADES OF GRAY

Macdonald
Queen Anne Press

Acknowledgement
Many thanks to Tim Russon without whom
this book would not have been possible.

A **Queen Anne Press** BOOK

© Andy Gray 1986

First published in 1986 by Queen Anne Press,
a division of Macdonald & Co (Publishers) Ltd,
Greater London House, Hampstead Road, London NW1 7QX
A BPCC plc Company

British Library Cataloguing in Publication Data
Gray, Andy
    Shades of Gray
    1. Gray, Andy   2. Soccer players-Great Britain
    —Biography
    I. Title
    796.334'092'4   GV942.7.G6/

    ISBN 0-356-12222-0

Typeset by Cylinder Typesetting, London
Printed and bound in Great Britain by
Billing and Sons Limited, Worcester

For Janet and Amy

CONTENTS

1 THE SIGNING

Fearless, brave, courageous, defiant . . . he who dares . . . are just a few of the headlines that have followed me around on my football career. And the headlines were never bigger or bolder than the day the name of Andy Gray attracted all the eyes of the football world.

It was the day I signed for Wolverhampton Wanderers, for a then British record fee of £1,469,000; it was the biggest day in my football career, but it also was the day that so nearly brought the big time to a shattering finish. The record breaking transfer, which was back page news in every paper, and even front page in some, fell apart only an hour before I was due to sign for Wolves in front of thousands of fans at their Molineux ground. It was saved by an ultimatum from the Wolves manager John Barnwell who told his directors, "You either sign Andy Gray or I walk out here and now." What went wrong? Quite simple. I failed the medical.

Never before or since have I endured such a day. It started with feelings of expectation and excitement; later there was tension and shock followed by relief and rejoicing. It should have been the day I'd always dreamt of, and worked for, and I suppose in the end it was, but I could never go through it all again. Saturday, September 8th, 1979 will go down as one of the landmarks in the history of football when the transfer market was at its craziest. How could a kid from the depths of Drumchapel in Glasgow be worth so much money?

For lads like me football had always been the one salvation. It was the only chance we had to break down the barriers of our upbringing and make a living and a name for ourselves. Not

9

that we were ashamed of who we were or where we came from but ever since my early teens I had been determined to be different, to achieve something, and I always knew football was my only hope. It was that drive and determination, an undying love for the game, and some luck of course, that had brought me all the way to a record breaking transfer. Although the staggering fee was not preying on my mind, I can't deny the sense of achievement and fulfilment I felt the morning of that big move. And like any person on the verge of such a memorable day in their lives, my hopes for the future were mixed with some thoughts from the past. Football had always been the dominating force in my family. With three big brothers and every relative a declared and devoted fan of Glasgow Rangers and Scotland, one of the first real challenges in life had been to kick a football straight. Like any other kid I played in my own private pretend world where my dreams were of scoring goal upon goal for my beloved Rangers. Real life was a bit different though. I started out as a goalkeeper, mainly because I was the youngest and smallest in the family, was given little say in things and was forced to play twice as hard as anyone else just to survive. Every spare minute we had as kids was spent either playing or watching football. It was that extra effort and deep desire to win or more like a hatred of losing, which had pulled me through the ranks of schoolboy football to a professional career.

I must have been fifteen when I suddenly realised my soccer hopes could come true. As I played for the Scottish schoolboys the dream came closer, but just when I thought a golden future was assured I was rejected and branded as pathetic in my first big trial. That was with Dundee United, but only a few months later I was fighting back and at seventeen made my professional debut for them in the Scottish League Cup. I didn't know it then, but stepping out onto the football stage was like jumping on to a highland express. Andy Gray may have been a slow starter but once he was out of the station there was no stopping him. In my first season I finished up playing in the Scottish Cup Final against Glasgow Celtic and was voted Dundee United's player of the year. And in with the success there was the despair as well, as I fought the first of many injury battles.

In my second season I topped the goalscorers, was voted player of the year again and was picked to play for the Scotland under-23 team. When still only nineteen I was nearly snatched from British football by a top European side who wanted to make me the wealthiest teenager in the world. I could have become the first British player to hit the big time in Europe with an offer which even all these years later most players would jump at. A signing on fee of £100,000 and a contract worth £60,000 a year was mine for the taking. However, I turned my back on it because the most important thing then, as now, was to enjoy my football and achieve success in the country which to me has always been the capital of the game. I was frightened as well to leave my homeland and live in a strange country. What I wanted more than anything was to play in the English first division and it was Aston Villa who made those dreams come true when they paid a record £110,000 to ship me to Birmingham.

It was the start of a love affair, which like many relationships had its ups and downs. There was success as I was picked to play for Scotland at Hampden; and then a season later finished up as the leading marksman in the first division. Along the way there was a League Cup Final at Wembley, and a piece of soccer history when I became the only man to win both the Player and Young Player of the Year awards. I was hailed as the new Denis Law . . . the next Johan Cruyff . . . the most exciting young striker ever to grace the English game. My daredevil style earned me praise from such men as England managers Don Revie and Bobby Robson who thought I was one of the best things that had happened to English soccer in a long time; but there were critics as well. Another first division manager, John Bond, reckoned I wouldn't last above eighteen months and the man who signed me and then scrapped me, Ron Saunders, reckoned fame came too quickly. It was Saunders as well, the so-called iron man of Villa Park, who branded me a cheat and a chicken when injury forced me to miss one of the club's biggest matches in years; but it was for Saunders I had played time and time again when only half fit, had been pumped full of pain killers in order to limp into battle, and yet it was the Villa manager who finally made me leave the club I felt so much for.

The record breaking transfer may have brought delight to Wolves but it started a civil war at Villa Park which rumbled for years. Supporters demonstrated and protested for the club to keep me and even the Villa directors invited me to a secret session when they asked if I would stay if they got a new manager to replace Ron Saunders. I was accused of being disloyal to the club and yet years later I returned to Villa Park for half the money I could have earned on the continent . . . such was my devotion to the claret and blue.

Back in 1979 though, I was leading a charmed life. The ball always bounced my way and I was loving every minute of it, so the events of that September Saturday made me realise just how lucky I had been and eventually how fortunate I was.

The move to Wolves had only been on the boil, publically, for about a week, and although most of the negotiations had been finalised on the Friday, Wolves wanted to make a real show out of the signing so everything was stage managed. The plan was for me to have a routine medical in the morning and then sign on the pitch before the match with Crystal Palace. Television companies wanted to screen the signing but Wolves manager John Barnwell was determined the fans would enjoy it first and boldly declared, "Television offered money to show the signing live but Andy Gray now belongs to the people of Wolverhampton and they should be first to see the signing . . . we have made football history with this deal and I want our public to be involved in it." That was typical of John Barnwell who had the rare gift of being able to lift and motivate people with his words. The Wolverhampton football folk must have looked upon him as their crusader and his daring bid of more than a million pounds for me had set the town alive.

Despite all the excitement and the extra attention I managed to get a good night sleep before my big day and woke to a blaze of headlines and stories. "Gray is on his way" . . . "Gray Won't Wait" . . . "Gray signs on the pitch" . . . "Mi££ion-Heirs" . . . "A Gray Day" . . . were just a few of the headlines filling the back pages of the papers that morning.

My girlfriend Vanessa and I made for Molineux early and what a happy and lighthearted mood we were in. The last few weeks at Villa had been wrecked with controversy. The Andy Gray transfer saga, it seemed, was big news and hardly surprising when you consider the amount of money involved. Rumour had it I was short of cash and in trouble with the nightclub I ran in Birmingham; but money never entered into the move. Although Wolves were breaking the British record there was no fat pay rise for me. There was no backhander either because the deal was I'd sign for the same money I was getting with Villa and if in the first season proved both my fitness and my form there would be a rise in the following year.

The most important thing that Saturday morning was my fitness. I hadn't played for months and was still recovering from an operation, the third, on my right knee. So after arriving at Molineux I was whisked away to the specialist for an extra medical. After the usual X-rays the doctor must have spent a good fifteen minutes probing and prodding my knee. The scar tissue made it look like a battlefield, and I could tell immediately he was not happy with it. "Does it feel alright?" he asked, "Any pain or discomfort from it?" he wanted to know. "It's fine," I said "A little stiff, but that'll disappear when I start playing again won't it?"

After the medical it was back to the ground for a bite of lunch, a meeting with some of the club's directors and officials and then at around half past two I would be led out onto the pitch and sign the transfer forms . . . that was the plan anyway. As we made our way back to the club I could feel the excitement beginning to build inside me as we passed the first trickle of supporters making their way to the match. Wolves, of course, had been one of the early pioneers of European football, and in the great days of the fifties when Stan Cullis was manager and the ever reliable England centre half Billy Wright was captain, they had been invincible. In more recent years people have marvelled at the brilliance and consistency of such sides as Liverpool and Arsenal in the double year, Leeds under Don Revie, and of course in the last season or two, Everton, but Wolves in their day must have been every bit as good. In a golden decade they lifted three League Championships and two FA Cups and together with Manchester United led the charge into European competition. Names such as goalkeeper Bert Williams, defenders Bill Slater and Ron Flowers, and wingers Jimmy Mullen and Johnny Hancocks, were still regarded as heroes and rightly so. Since that era Wolves had been in decline with only one major victory to show in the past twenty years. That was perhaps why my signing meant so much to the club and had caused such a stir in the town. For too long the faithful who wore the old gold and black had been forced to live on memories. Even the young lads had been brought up on tales of yesteryear, as the present day Wolves struggled to stay afloat in the first division. The arrival of Britain's most expensive player was supposed to be the start of a new era . . . an era when Wolves would recapture some of their old glory and teams would shudder once more at the thought of playing at Molineux. And, it seemed as though the signing was working that Saturday lunchtime. The nearer we got to the ground, the thicker the crowds got. Once more the faithful were out in force. There was a buzz around the whole place and everyone wanted to meet, greet and shake the hand of Andy Gray.

The Molineux stadium, standing just down from the town centre and lying off the main ring-road, has always been one of the best known local landmarks. Most of the ground had not changed since the fifties when crowds of forty or fifty thousand were commonplace. The only big change in recent years had been the development of a new £2.5 million stand opened just a few weeks before my arrival as further proof that the club was planning and preparing for a successful future. Walking into the main entrance at Molineux was like stepping back in time because you could not avoid the reminders of those great days. In the main foyer a trophy cupboard was stacked high with silver cups and momentoes and lined with pennants. Most of them had been won by the likes of Wright and Mullen and almost at once I realised one of my main tasks was to help build a more modern collection.

Despite the vast amount of money involved, the actual transfer negotiations between us had taken practically no time at all, and it was just a question of dotting the i's and crossing the t's. After all when you are sitting at a table in the middle of the pitch with thousands of excited fans watching on, and scores of photographers waiting to pounce, there's not much chance to raise any last worries. I had no worries mind you, because I was convinced the move to Wolves was the right one. My time at Villa had been enjoyable and unforgettable, and the fans in particular had always been marvellous, but for one reason or another I knew the time was right to move. It had been suggested a bigger club, such as Liverpool, might come in and buy me, but I was content. I was going to be happy at Molineux where the future looked exciting. In John Barnwell Wolves had a likeable, ambitious and capable manager. We'd hit it off at our very first meeting and his conviction that Wolves were a team on the move seemed to be shared by everyone around him.

When John Barnwell greeted us on that Saturday though I could sense something was not quite right. He was always a bouncy and bubbly kind of figure and earlier his obvious pride at having a hand in football history and providing Wolves with their biggest day in years had been beaming like a beacon. Now he looked more drawn and serious as he ushered Vanessa and I into his office. His office at Molineux must have been one of the pokiest in the entire football league. Managers may get paid a lot of money but not all have the luxuries you are sometimes led to believe. In John Barnwell's office there was room for his desk, a cabinet and a couple of chairs. It was under the old main stand and the ceiling sloped down. Up above you could hear the rumble of fans making their way to the seats. Along the side of the front wall at the very top were narrow reinforced coloured glass windows which opened out onto the ground. As we sat in the office the noise from the terraces came flooding through and got noisier by the minute. Vanessa and I sat down facing John Barnwell and whether it was intuition or not I knew exactly what he was going to say. "I'm afraid we've hit a bit of a problem Andy," Barnwell said "It's your knee. The specialist has had a long look at it this morning and after studying the X-rays he's not very happy. To be honest he's recommending we call the whole deal off." I could sense that Barnwell was searching my face for some reaction. What could I say? I was stunned into silence and just as I was about to mumble a few words of shock Barnwell burst in again. "We'll sort something out lad. I know you're fit and so do you for Christ sake. I hope this knee is just a minor detail. You see with so much money riding on the deal the doctor is obviously being a bit more cautious than usual and the board are getting cold feet. They're worried about the insurance angle but never fear lad we'll be off out to do the business in a minute. I'll sort something out." And with that the Wolves manager got up and made his way down the corridor to confront his directors.

My mind was racing now with panic. I'd always had a nagging doubt about my knee and knew as soon as I'd seen John Barnwell that afternoon there was trouble ahead. Deep down I knew, or rather I was trying to convince myself I was all right, but at the same time I knew as well of other players before me who had been stopped from moving by medicals. I thought immediately of another Scottish lad, Asa Hartford, whose £177,000 move to Leeds United in November 1971 had been blocked when doctors discovered he had a hole in the heart. At the time the transfer, like mine now, was the talk of football and I can remember reading and being told how Asa was all set to play for Leeds, who were then of course the top team in the country, until the verdict from the medical examination had ruined everything for him. It was not as serious as first thought thankfully, and Asa had since proved he was as fit and as fiery as the next man. At the time though it must have been a nightmare for him. Could such a thing be happening to me I thought, as I sat and sweated for what seemed like an eternity. For a time I was convinced I would be going back to Villa Park. That didn't hurt because in some ways I was sorry to be leaving there. What did hurt was the thought of having to walk from Molineux that afternoon when so many people were expecting me out there to sign. And more than anything I dreaded the prospect of being labelled a reject. If the deal fell through, then everywhere I went and every match I played in I'd feel I'd be under the microscope and fearing the first tackle or knock on my knee. "There goes Andy Gray . . . what a good player he was . . . shame about the knee . . ." These were the words that were burning in my brain. What if the doctor was right and my knee

was suspect. Would it mean me dropping out of the first division
. . . another operation perhaps? . . . or worst of all, could my
whole career be threatened?

That half an hour wait below the stand at Molineux was the
worst of my life. The manager's office was like the condemned
cell that Saturday lunchtime as I prayed for the return of John
Barnwell with some better news.

Then I heard John Barnwell's voice booming outside and his
unmistakeable chuckle of laughter. He practically knocked the
door down and as soon as I saw his face I knew the signing was
back on. "They are still a bit worried but I've managed to
convince them. I told them straight if they didn't go ahead with
the deal after this, they'd not only be looking for another striker
but would need a new manager as well," he said. "It's not every
day you make history and anyway we've got a few thousand
fans waiting for us out there. But whatever you do, don't
breathe a word about this to anyone," said Barnwell. "Don't be
daft," I said "I'm the last one who's going to go shouting about
the doc's verdict on my knee."

I was thankful it had all happened before a match. Ever
since, I've wondered what would have been the decision of the
Wolves board if the signing had not been planned in public.
Would they have backed down, sent me back to Aston Villa and
spent the money on someone else? With over 24,000 people in
the ground that Saturday and Molineux the focus of attention,
they must have been under pressure and thought if there was a
gamble it was worth taking it there and then. What had finally
swayed them? . . . the crowd outside, or John Barnwell's ultimatum? Nobody ever told me and strange as it might seem the
medical was never talked of again. But I've always wondered
what would have happened if the deal had fallen through and
I'd gone back to Aston Villa branded as a reject. Up until then
everything had gone well, but I was still only twenty-three and
little did I know at the time that the best, in many ways, was still
to come.

You can never predict a footballer's career. That first season
at Molineux I think I justified Wolves' faith in me by scoring
the winning goal in the League Cup Final at Wembley against

Nottingham Forest, a victory which also took the club back into European football. The next but one season though we dropped into the second division for a year, as the club, saddled with debts, escaped bankruptcy by a whisker. I was nearly sold for a million pounds again, and finally when I left for Everton four years later I went for £200,000, a seventh of the fee Wolves had paid for me. There were some then who even thought that was too much because Andy Gray was past his best and the goals had dried up. I wondered with them at times, but I knew there was still some of that old drive and determination left. In all honesty, although I never gave up hope, I didn't think I'd be in a team that would win the FA Cup, the League Championship and European Cup Winners Cup all in the space of twelve months.

Looking back to that day at Molineux it could all have been different. The rest of the afternoon was like a carnival, and despite the torment of the failed medical I was happier than I'd been for ages. Before signing I did a round of interviews with local and national radio stations although I didn't tell them a word about what had been going on. The press all thought I'd been taken out for lunch and then across to the new stand to meet some of the club's more influential followers. If only they had known the real truth!

I signed hundreds of autographs as I fought my way to and from the press box which was tucked away at the back of the stand and shook about twice as many hands. It was great to see so much happiness on so many faces and it was now up to me and the rest of my new teammates at Wolves to fulfil some of their long held dreams. After the interviews it was time for the ceremony. John Barnwell and I walked down the long corridor past the dressing rooms, where you could hear the clatter of the player's boots as they prepared themselves for the game, and then a sharp right and we were in the mouth of the Molineux tunnel. As we emerged a deafening cheer engulfed us, all around people were waving and shouting. Black and gold banners and scarves flowed in the wind and the chant from all four corners of the ground was Andy Gray. Every photographer in Fleet Street was there along with the television cameras who shoved and bustled with each other to get the best pictures. The actual signing was all over in a second or two; it was the most expensive bit of paper I'll ever sign in my life and I could not wait to get my name on the dotted line. John Barnwell stood by my side and as I signed he raised his fingers in an Churchillian victory salute. That was the signal for another roar of delight from the crowd. Then we went on a lap of honour as those in the seats stood and applauded. The new stand was just about full and away to one end the famous South Bank, where in Wolves' heyday as many as 30,000 fans would gather, was awash with colour. What marvellous scenes they were and the only disappointment was that I had to watch the game from the director's box. Given the chance though, I would have loved to slip on my boots and pull on a Wolves shirt there and then, and gone out to score a goal to prove to Wolves and myself that the knee was as strong as ever.

On that September day I was sworn to secrecy about the amazing dilemma of the record deal. I don't know what was said then, or has been said since by others, but there were always rumours about my medical. I was asked quite a few times whether it was true I had failed the fitness test and I suspected that one or two outside Molineux knew what really did happen. Until now I've never told the whole truth. When I think about it I just count my blessings that John Barnwell and Wolves had faith in my future. I like to think I repaid them for it, and also helped provide the Wolves fans with a few more memories. Although it was a day of history and high drama, it was just one of many unforgettable moments in the football life of Andy Gray.

2 DRUMCHAPEL DAYS

Life began for me on November 30th, 1955. And the amazing thing is that virtually every true Scot alive was raising a glass that night to toast another Andrew . . . St. Andrew. Much to the delight of the Gray clan I was born on the day of Scotland's patron saint and so my mother did not have to look far for the right name. The family though, have always told me that her joy of having a son on St. Andrew's Day was a mixed blessing. With three sons already my Mum, Margaret, had set her heart on a daughter. When I came along she cried, some say in delight, others in disappointment and ever since I've pulled her leg about how she rejected me at birth. Nothing, of course could be further from the truth, as the youngest in the family I always had a special place.

I was born and brought up in Drumchapel, a large council estate which sprawls across the outskirts of Glasgow. It's well known in Scotland, but sadly not for its natural beauty. The estate is one of the toughest areas you could find north, or come to that south of the border. Comedians will tell you Drumchapel is such a hard area even the alsatians go round in pairs. The best description I've ever heard comes from one of Scotland's most famous sons, Billy Connolly, another old inmate of the estate. He called it a desert with windows.

So, Drumchapel was not the sort of place you would dream of living, but to the Gray family, Lillyburn Place was, and still is, a very happy family home. We lived at number 15, a ground floor flat, and never let it be said the Gray family did not go up in the world. When we moved, we went to number 17, on the fourth floor! My father, William, left home when I was two, so Mum was left with the task of caring for and controlling four boys. Willie was the eldest, and when Dad left home he was forced to give up his studies and leave school early in order to find a job and earn much needed money for the home. He was twelve years older than me; then came James who was nine years older – he was quieter and more of a studious type; and then there was Duncan, who was still five years older than me. He was the most fiery of us all, and if ever there was any trouble or complaints coming the Gray's way, you could bet that somewhere along the line our Duncan was involved.

I took after James more than the other two, and my Mum always reckoned that we would be the white collar workers, while Duncan and Willie would be the black collar workers. In my younger days I looked upon big brother Willie as the father of the family. Together with Mum, he was in charge of discipline, and helped to keep us all out of any serious trouble. Mum was what is called a teuchter, in Scotland, a lass from the Isle of Lewis in the Outer Hebrides. She was fiercely proud of her boys, deeply religous, hardworking and strict. With so many troublemakers and apprentice gangsters around in Drumchapel, it would have been easy for four fatherless boys to drift into a life of crime. My Mum and big Willie made sure we behaved ourselves, and the slightest act of disobedience would bring a clip round the ear.

Between them Mum and Willie did us proud. Willie worked as a gas fitter, while Mum toiled away as a cleaner and a cook at the local school on the estate. She worked all hours from first thing in the morning to last thing at night to earn enough money, and Sunday was her only day off. We had very little money and as the youngest I felt the full force. Most of my clothes were hand-me-downs, and you can imagine what sort of state they were in when they finally fitted me! They used to say that Andrew Gray was the scruffiest but best loved kid in Drumchapel. I only had one set of clothes of my very own . . . my Sunday best, and the first time I can remember feeling the ferocious force of Mum's temper was all down to those. It was a Sunday and for me that meant church. Mum got me changed into my best clothes and then told me to wait for her outside while she got ready. My Mum was a long time coming, so off I went exploring by a local stream which ran through the estate. I slipped and fell in and will never forget the look on my mother's face when she found me lying on my back in the water in my Sunday best. It was a thick ear and early to bed that night, and that unfortunate incident just about sums up my childhood in Drumchapel. I was never a troublemaker because, luckily, along with my brothers, I fell in with the right bunch of lads. But I was still prone to getting into a few scrapes every now and then.

Life though for us Gray boys was really about one thing . . . football. All our effort and enthusiasm was channelled into the game. We played every day either at school or around home and the biggest treat of the week came on a Saturday with a trip to town to watch the mighty Glasgow Rangers play at Ibrox Stadium. In Drumchapel, like anywhere else in Glasgow, you supported either Rangers or Celtic. Most of the "old firm" fervour was based on religion. The Protestants wore the blue of Rangers and the Roman Catholics the Celtic green and it was unheard of for anyone to switch sides. You often find in other famous football cities that support can be scattered amongst folk. When I played in Birmingham I knew of several families that were split by their football favourites. Dad, and one of the boys say, would support Aston Villa, while Mum would carry the flag for Birmingham City. The same thing can happen in Liverpool between Everton and Anfield followers, but in Glasgow you were born either a Rangers fan or a Celtic supporter. They like to joke up there that allegiance should even be stated on your birth certificate, because for so many people, football is life itself.

Rivalry between the two teams and their supporters is part of Scottish history and I can tell you two tales of how much it means. One of my biggest treats as a kid came on a Wednesday when Mum would pick up her wage packet from the school. Each and every week she would call into the local shop on her way home to buy a packet of six penguin biscuits. Chocolate biscuits once a week were one of the few luxuries we indulged in, and most Wednesday's I'd be sitting on the step waiting for

Mum to come the street. Now there were six biscuits in the packet and each one was wrapped in brightly coloured foil. When Mum undid the packet, the fight was on between me and my brothers to get the one in the blue Rangers wrapper. And would you believe every week, the one that was left had a green Celtic wrapper. Football was all very important. My other story comes from a Christmas. A pal of mine, Eddie Hayes, had spent most of Christmas Eve decorating the family home with brightly coloured balloons. They were hanging from every ceiling in the house, and made the place look very festive. When his Dad, an ardent Rangers man, arrived home from work though there was trouble. The whole family watched in disbelief as the old man dived into the sewing box and armed with a pin went round the house bursting every green balloon he could find.

The Grays then were for Rangers, and on the Drumchapel estate most of our schoolboy soccer matches ended up as local derbies. There was a good spread of boys from both camps and you could be sure of one thing where we lived, there was always a soccer game going on somewhere. Our pitch was on a green in the middle of the estate. We used jackets or sticks for goalposts, and someone always had a ball. So hour upon hour was spent playing soccer. My three big brothers, who till this very day I declare were all better players than me, taught me everything they knew about the game, and training started when I was just five. When Mum left for work after tea Willie was put in charge, and no sooner was the door shut behind her than the furniture was quickly re-arranged so we could play football. As the youngest and the smallest I was always put in goal. I could just about stand up between the table legs and that's where my football career really started. Because of my brothers I always used to end up playing with lads much older and bigger, and that meant game after game in goal. My Mum loves to tell the tale of how I would run home with tears streaming down my cheeks because the other lads would not let me play out. She would grab me by the hand, march me back to the field and order them to let her Andrew, as she always called me, have a shoot at goal. For a few minutes it would work, as I got my chance to get more involved with the action, but as soon as she had disappeared around the corner, back in goal I would go. After a time I quite got to like playing in goal and would see myself at Ibrox defying the charge of the green and white hooped shirts of the enemy Celtic. My uncle used to play with us during the summer holidays and if I let in a goal he would call me Frank Haffey, after the Celtic keeper, but if I saved the ball then my name was Billy Ritchie, who was of course the Rangers goalie in the early sixties.

Those summer holidays were, perhaps, the happiest of my childhood. Every year we would pack up and make for my grandparents' home on the Isle of Lewis. The journey was an adventure in itself, as it was the only time we ever went anywhere. We would leave home at four in the morning and catch the train from Glasgow to Mallaig, a trip which took six hours. Then it was onto the steamer for another six hours and what a great sight it was each summer to see the town of Stornoway on the horizon. The crofters' cottages, the fishermens' nets and boats and the tweedweaving sheds provided such a warm change from the cast concrete of Drumchapel.

We went as a family with some cousins as well and after twelve hours of travelling it was good to get there. I was always desperately hungry on those journies to and from the Isle of Lewis. All the kids would have packs of sandwiches and I was a greedy so and so. I would gollup mine down in the first five minutes and spend the rest of the trip trying to beg or borrow crumbs from everybody else.

My Grandpa and Grandma Murray lived in the tiny village of Back on the island. They had built the first house there and my Grandpa was one of the elders of the local community. As village blacksmith and school caretaker he knew everyone young and old for miles around . . . and they all knew him, of course. We would spend all eight weeks of our school summer holidays on the island and there's many a time when I could have stayed in Back for good.

Sadly, September saw us back to school in Glasgow and the first seat of learning for Andy Gray was Lochgoin Primary on the Drumchapel estate. I was one of those kids that all through school managed to get by without really having to work too hard at it. In class I always did fairly well and enjoyed getting things right . . . I suppose it was the start of my competitive spirit. I was the only kid in the class who could spell beautifully; not much of an achievement I know, but at the time it gave me great satisfaction.

For me though, lessons were only the intervals between our football games. Before school, during the breaks and then again after lessons, we would devote all our time to playing soccer. There was a strict code of conduct at school as well. The top class, the oldest boys, were allowed to play on the pitch, while all the others had to share the playground. In my younger days that meant there were six or seven games all going on together and the biggest battle was often to find a way through the crowds. When it came to our turn to play on the pitch, what games we had, and happily the school team that year finished off as champions of all Glasgow, and that was my first football honour. Surprisingly, my first coach was a lady. Sandra McArthur, a teacher at Lochgoin primary, was the only person interested in looking after the football team, and she was very kind to us all. Her best qualification was being able to drive the team coach, the school mini-bus, to and from matches. She never got involved with the tactics or training, as the team picked itself. At nights and at weekends we would play on the local pitch and one of the worst times for me came on a Sunday. In the morning I was out early to find a game to play in and I would dread hearing my mother calling me home to get changed for Sunday school. The worst of it was that I would have to walk past the pitch to church and the other lads, who were older and didn't have to go to Sunday school, would rib me unmercifully as I strode by in my best clothes with my hair carefully combed and parted. There came a time when the lure of football would prove too much, and after changing into my best clothes I would run off to find a game of soccer to play in rather than go to church. Mum must have been suspicious when she saw the state of my clothers at night, but the real crunch came when my attendance card arrived from the church and there were no ticks on it. The truth came out and although it brought a telling off, Mum realised I was too big to be ordered off to school every

Sunday and so from then on I devoted all my weekend to football.

Saturday was the highlight in my younger days, because Willie, James and Duncan would take me with them to watch Rangers play at Ibrox. We'd catch the number 19 bus to Govan and from there the ground was a forty-five minute walk. In those days we would be swept along on a tide of blue as we made for the great stadium and I'm ashamed to say that most of my matches at Ibrox did not cost me a penny. Willie or one of my elder brothers would quickly lift me over the turnstiles and I'd run off into the crowd and meet up with them inside. Many is the time I went to Ibrox alone or with some friends of my own age with only enough money for the bus fare home in my pocket. Then we would search for a kind looking chap to lift us over the turnstiles into the ground. It worked nearly every time and we never got caught. At Ibrox we always stood behind the goal in the Rangers end at gate number 13. In the early sixties Scottish football was totally dominated by the two great Glasgow teams. They virtually took it in turns to win the league and the cup, and when I was eight Rangers won the double two years running.

In those days Rangers were at their very best. The names I can remember are the all-time greats like Jim Baxter, one of the most stylish and skilful of players ever to pull on the blue shirt. There were the wingers Willie Henderson and Davie Wilson, and in defence John Greig never ever put a foot wrong. Although I worshipped all the players and the teams as a kid, the first professional player who really caught my eye was a young centre forward who arrived at Ibrox in October 1968. By this time I was nearing my thirteenth birthday and I suppose was more aware of football skills. The player who captured my imagination was Colin Stein who Rangers had bought from the Edinburgh club, Hibernian, for £100,000, which was the first six figure transfer deal between two Scottish clubs. He arrived in Glasgow with a reputation for getting goals. The papers, which I always read as I made my delivery rounds in Drumchapel, said he had the qualities of a classic centre-forward. He had tenacity, skill on the ball, was an intelligent runner and had a deadly shot with either foot. I can remember watching Colin Stein making his debut at Ibrox and what a game he played. To the delight of every Rangers fan he slammed home a hat-trick and was every bit as good as the rave reviews he had been given. Stein, in fact, scored eight goals in his first three matches for Rangers which included two hat-tricks. From then on my mind was made up, I wanted to be a dashing centre forward and a goal grabber like Colin Stein.

The Rangers matches also evoke other memories . . . sadder ones of my boyhood, as it was at Ibrox that I got to know my father for the first time. Because he left home when I was a toddler I never really knew what had gone wrong between Mum and him, and it wasn't a subject on which we often spoke. My older brothers, especially Willie, who had been given the extra responsibility, were, I think, a little cold towards him and Dad was rarely mentioned at home. When I was about nine he started taking me to Rangers matches on a Saturday. In all the years he never once came to our home in Drumchapel and we would always meet in town. I used to catch a bus into Glasgow and meet him outside a pub near Ibrox. We got on well but sadly never had a real father and son relationship. He drifted out of my life when I was about thirteen but then in later years enjoyed coming to watch me play with Dundee United and Aston Villa.

He died while I was at Villa Park and the last and saddest memory I have of my Dad was seeing him for the last time in hospital. For several months he'd been fighting cancer and had undergone the usual course of radiation treatment. When I went to see him, on a trip home, he didn't look too bad although I knew, and I'm sure he did as well, that he was dying. I sat and chatted by his bed and then just as I got up to go I asked him if there was anything he wanted. "There is one thing Andrew," he said. "All my life I've always wanted to shave with one of those electric razors. I've never been able to get one and I've often wondered what they were like." It seemed a strange request but a sad one, so I went straight out of the hospital and found the nearest electrical shop where I bought the best razor they had for my Dad. I took it back and he was delighted with it.

I never got to know whether he used it and in a way I don't think I really wanted to know because at the time I was humbled. The electric razor was the only thing my Dad ever asked me for; soon afterwards he died. I knew he was proud of me playing football for Scotland, and when I think of him now I always look back to that hospital visit and his dying wish. If it was my Dad's love of football I inherited then I owe him a lot, although to be fair Willie, my brother, was more of a father to me and was always there when I needed help or advice.

But when it came to football James was the real inspiration. When he left school he turned professional with Clydebank which was the nearest team to Drumchapel. James was a right winger and had a couple of seasons in the Scottish League. He used to take me to most of the home matches and what's more I was allowed into the dressing room. I was only about ten then and would make myself useful by pouring cups of tea for the players at half-time and clearing up after them at the end. James, potentially, was a good player. His temper let him down though, and he was forever getting sent off which really used to get Mum angry. He packed it up after a couple of seasons and went to live in Canada where he has been happily settled ever since with a good steady job as an insurance adjuster over there.

My other brother Duncan was the one who really threw his football career away. I will never forget the time he was selected to play for the Glasgow under-18 boys team, quite an achievement. Duncan was a wonderfully gifted midfield player, the best of us all I think, and had been told to catch the team bus in the city centre at ten o'clock one Saturday morning. At 10.15 the phone went at home. Duncan had not turned up and the Glasgow boys were having to leave without him. Mum checked his room and found his bed had not been slept in. Around lunchtime Duncan wandered in and Mum demanded to know where he had been and why he had not caught the team bus that morning. Duncan had been to an all night party and was having such a good time there, he did not feel like playing for the Glasgow boys side. I thought he was absolutely crazy and can remember trying to puzzle it out how anyone could throw away such a football chance, but that was Duncan. He simply lost interest in the game after that, although the funny thing is, now he will travel miles to watch a match and is absolutely mad about soccer.

In the meantime, I had moved on to the Kingsridge Secondary School, which was still in Drumchapel, where I was progressing well with both my studies and my football. I was a regular in the school team at number nine and it was now I began to realise how strong my determination and drive to win was. The thought of losing haunted me and I was so desperate to win every game that I ran twice as fast and twice as hard as any other player. My extra competitiveness began to bring results in goals for the school, and it also earned me a trial, and eventually a place in the Glasgow district team.

An old school pal of mine, John Smith, who was with me in class from the very start to the finish, still takes great delight in reminding me of how determined I used to be. When it came to picking sides for games I would invariably be nominated as one of the captains and all the lads used to try to push their way into my team. John reckons now that everyone wanted to be in my team because nine times out of ten it won, although I can remember one young goalkeeper who would not perhaps be all that keen to volunteer again for the Andy Gray eleven. We were playing a so-called friendly game at school and as usual I was one of the skippers. This shy, skinny lad had been put in goal in my team and after only a few minutes of the match let in a really soft goal. I was fuming and chased back to give him a piece of my mind. Grabbing hold of his jersey I hauled him towards me and snarled at him, "If you dare let any more goals like that one in today, I'll see you out of school later, O.K.?" And with that warning threw him back between the sticks. The poor lad went white with fright and about five minutes later I heard a tiny voice shouting from defence. It was the keeper, "Andrew, I've had my turn in goal, can I come out now?" Apparently he was absolutely terrified of letting in another goal which would bring him a beating up after school from me. I wasn't a bully at school and laugh about it now. Fancy threatening to fight someone for just letting in a goal in a friendly game. It shows though, just how seriously I took winning even then, and there is no doubt it was that unrivalled will to win that lifted me above most of my mates and gave me the chance to have a crack at the big time.

By the time I was fifteen my mind was really made up . . . I was going to be a professional footballer. I'd also grown a lot and shot up about six inches in a year which gave me the strength to challenge for that ambition of mine. My teachers at school, were having other thoughts, expecially when I fared so well in the 'O' level exams. Much to my suprise, and a few others I might add, I passed in no fewer than eight subjects which meant I could go on to sit my highers and perhaps try for a place at college.

My heart though was set on football, so much so it led to a confrontation with a local careers officer, which is still talked of in Glasgow to this day. The officer from the city's education department was making one of her usual visits to the school to help and advise us on what sort of jobs we could look forward to and prepare for on leaving the sixth form. Now, most lads spent between twenty and thirty minutes with the careers officer discussing this or that, and finally it came to my turn. I walked in the room where the careers officer was surrounded by books, pamphlets and forms. There was everything there from the army to architecture and she was quite a friendly sort of person who enjoyed helping youngsters on their way. "Now Andrew Gray isn't it? You've got eight 'O' levels which is very good and are taking four more exams next summer. Have you got any ideas on what you'd like to do when you leave school?" she said. Without a moments hesitation I replied, "Oh yes miss . . . it's all fixed, I've decided I'm going to be a professional footballer." Well that absolutely threw her. She had no answer to it and she could see how determined I was. "Well if you're sure Andrew, then there's nothing I can really help you with is there? All I can say is good luck." And that was my careers interview. I was in and out inside two minutes . . . a Kingsridge Secondary all-comers record. All the other pupils had emerged from their interviews with armfuls of pamphlets and literature and I had walked out with only a smile. My mates were surprised to see me emerge so soon. "What are you going to be Andy? What did she tell you?" they asked. "Told her the truth didn't I? That I was going to be a professional soccer player." They looked about as stunned as the careers officer and the word soon got round the rest of the school. So as far as I was concerned, my future was settled. It was football for me.

THE KICK-OFF

The year of 1972 brought an Indian summer to the highlands of Scotland, and so happy were the Gray family on their yearly trip to the Isle of Lewis that time could have stood still for ever. By now it was just Mum and I making the summer trip to the family home in Back where there were uncles and aunts and countless cousins. It was the last real summer we had together as a family and it turned out to be one of the most eventful; for amazingly it was in the Outer Hebrides, which always seemed like a million miles from the football fervour of Glasgow, that I won my first league and cup double. The village soccer team in Back had been struggling for players over the years and word went round that the young Gray boy who was stopping with his grandparents was a fair player. So they asked me to join the team that summer along with another boy from the city who was stopping there as well, in the hope they might win a few more matches. Lewis may be an outpost, but they still enjoyed their football and the league, which was contested by teams from all the island's tiny villages, was quite competitive. The pitch in Back had been hewn out of the sand dunes and there were no facilities other than a set of goalposts.

We changed in cars, and after the matches, win or lose, refreshments were bought in the local village pub. It had been twenty-five years or so since Back had done well in the league, but that summer the team enjoyed its best run for ages. I played at centre forward and got amongst the goals, and by the end of the season we were on the verge of winning the league and cup double. The championship was decided on the last Saturday of the league season and in a play-off, Back were up against a team called Lochs. At half-time you could have got odds of a 1000-1 of us winning the title as we went in losing 3-0 with the match all but lost. The second half, though, was quite different, and in one of the best comebacks I've played in from that day to this we drew level and forced the match into extra time. I was praying someone would score and happily Back just managed it.

So with the league championship in the bag, our next target was the Isle of Heather Cup. In the final Back were to play the village of Point, who were their arch rivals from a long way back. It was, I suppose, the nearest the Isle of Lewis got to a local derby. The only snag was by now the summer holidays had finished and I had to return to school in Glasgow. Back, though, were desperate for victory in the final and they decided to spend the club funds on flying me and another Glasgow lad, Allan Kerr, from Glasgow to Stornaway on the weekend of the big match with Point. I felt ten feet tall, of course. Fancy a team wanting to go to all that trouble to get me in their side. The air fare cost around £50 in those days and after school on the Friday, off I went from Glasgow airport for my first big final and my very first flight in a plane. I was so looking forward to the cup final that I forgot to worry about flying and the journey seemed an awful lot easier and more comfortable than the marathon train and steamer journeys I was used to. Not all of the Back team were happy though, about spending so much money on flying in a "foreigner" to play in their Isle of Heather Cup. I qualified for the team because I had relatives in the village, but I knew there were a couple of players who thought of me as an outsider and a waste of money. To make matters even worse the cup final finished in a draw on the Saturday with Andy Gray getting the equaliser which forced a replay, and that could not be played until the following week. It also meant Back had to fork out another £50 for the following weekend as Allan and I flew in again from Glasgow. Two thousand people, practically the whole village, lined the touchline for the replay as Back and Point battled it out once more. There must have been a few angry looks in my direction as well as we trailed 1-0 at half-time and looked to be heading for a humiliating defeat. I could just imagine what some of the other players must have been thinking about wasting their money on bringing me and Allan all the way from Glasgow to get beaten. We did them proud in the end mind you. I got the equaliser to force the match into extra time and Allan hit the winner, to take the cup.

There were some celebrations in Back that night and apparently, the year they won the league and cup double is still fondly remembered and recalled. My Mum was absolutely delighted I'd managed to help her home village to victory and two of her most treasured possesions are the medals, inscribed in Gaelic, which I won that year. And strange though it may sound, those medals have always been lucky ones for me because, from the Isle of Heather Cup Final, my football career snowballed.

Back in Glasgow I was selected to play for the Scottish schoolboys team against England at Partick Thistle's Firhill Ground and scored in a 2-1 defeat. Within weeks I was in the side again to play Wales at Tredegar, which meant my first football trip away from home. We were all given special suits to wear with a crest on the jacket pocket, and how proud I was as I walked down Lillyburn Place in my new Scottish uniform. Scotland lost the match to Wales 1-0 and although the result was a bitter disappointment, the occasion was a memorable one.

Another big break came when I was asked by a good pal of mine, Brian Paton who lived just across the road, whether I was interest in playing for the local juvenile side, Clydebank Strollers. He played for them, and one Saturday they found themselves short of a couple of players. Now in those days I was a fairly shy and quiet lad, and only went along to Clydebank because I knew Brian well. Had I not known anyone in the team, I would have been too frightened to go along on my own, because most of the lads were much older and more confident than me. So, off I went with Brian to the Strollers and much to my suprise was put straight into the team, when all along I expected to be substitute. It was my second game of the day, having turned out for the school in a league match in the morning. But as a sixteen-year-old energy and enthusiasm are things you are never short of, and my debut for the Strollers finished in a victory and a goal for me. From then on I was a regular in the team, and we enjoyed a fabulous run, including a memorable cup final win over our biggest rivals Kilbowie Union. We beat them 3-2 and the old Gray goal magic worked again. I got two of them, which helped me gain even further recognition. Shortly afterwards I was picked to play for the Scotland Amateur Youth side and then the Scottish juvenile team, and was lucky enough to score for both. It seemed I couldn't put a foot wrong.

It was while I was playing for the Strollers that a chap called Maurice Friel came back into my life and helped give me the biggest break of all. Maurice had been the physiotherapist and trainer with Clydebank when my older brother James was playing there, and knew the family. One night, he phoned me at home, and out of the blue asked if I would like to go for a trial with Dundee United, the first division side. Apparently, he had been monitoring my progress over the years, and had watched me several times from the touchline. It was my performances for the Strollers that had really impressed him, and his brief from Dundee United was to send up any lads who had potential. Although hundreds of boys are offered and given trials by professional clubs each year, I must admit my first reaction to the invitation was that I'd made it. I couldn't say yes quick enough to Maurice's offer, and so it was arranged shortly after my seventeenth birthday in December 1972, I would travel up to United's Tannadice Park home for a trial. The only time Maurice could arrange for me to go was during the school term and that meant, instead of spending a week up there like all the other triallists, I could only have one day.

It was a day I would love to forget. It should have been, or I was hoping it would be, of course, one of the best days of my life, but it was nearly the end of all those football dreams. The day itself was a typical dark and damp December one, when you get up, draw the curtains and feel like going straight back to bed. I was hoping my big brother Willie would come up to Dundee with me because the only instructions I had from Maurice Friel were to catch the train in Glasgow and then jump in a taxi at Dundee station and make for Tannadice. Although I was seventeen, I was still very shy and don't mind admitting I was scared by the thought of making such a journey on my own. I got there all right, and reported, as told, to the United manager Jim McLean who was thankfully expecting me and knew who I'd played for and what I'd done. "Good to see you laddie . . . slip down to the dressing room and get your boots on. We've a game between the first team and the reserves this morning. You can have a go in that," was how Jim McLean greeted me.

Right from that moment I was completely overawed by it all. I crept into the first team dressing room and burrowed into a corner to change, not daring to say a word to anyone. My hands were shaking so much it took twice as long as usual to tie my boots and all the time I felt as though all the other players, the senior pros, were watching my every move. I'm sure they didn't even notice me, either in the dressing room or out on the pitch where I played about the worst game in my life. Nerves, I suppose, had a lot to do with it, but here I was, a kid from the Glasgow schools and juvenile league being thrown into a full blooded first team versus second team practice match, which as I've discovered since, is sometimes tougher than the real thing. I touched the ball twice and felt nothing but relief when the whistle finally went. During the match I must have looked totally out of my depth, and at one stage when I saw Jim McLean scratching his head, I wondered if he thought he'd been sent the wrong young player. I must admit, for a moment, I wondered what I was doing there and my illusions were totally shattered as I walked off the pitch. I'd been out run, out manouevered and outplayed, and I'd thought after all the goals for the Strollers it was going to be much easier.

I disappeared back into the corner of the dressing room and managed to hide my shame in the steam from the piping hot baths and showers. Jim McLean saw me a few minutes after I'd changed. He thanked me for coming all the way from Glasgow and said they would keep a watch on me back in Drumchapel to see how I developed. He was very pleasant about it, but nevertheless, I took it to be a case of "Don't call us . . . we'll call you."

I walked out of Tannadice on that December day and for the first time in my life was totally devastated. My hopes, ambitions and dreams had been cruelly killed there that morning and, as I made for the station, I was convinced I would never become a professional footballer. What could I tell the careers officer now I thought as I made the long journey back home to Glasgow. To make it worse, my Mum and Willie were waiting for me, and it was desperately hard to tell them how badly I had done. I suppose they expected to see me bouncing through the door with a contract in my hand and a return ticket to Tannadice. Instead, there was a long unhappy face and a load of excuses. Jim McLean told me a few years later there was only one word he could use to sum up my trial match, and that was "pathetic". So how did I change his mind? I went back to Clydebank Strollers and to the school team and just kept plugging away. Little did I know at the time, but Maurice Friel was still watching me from time to time, and was trying his hardest to persuade Dundee United to give me another chance. Jim McLean did not want to know after my first trial and Maurice phoned him every week with reports of the goals I had scored in various matches.

Then, in the New Year of 1973, I was chosen to play for the Scottish Professional Youth side. All the other players in the team were with top sides such as Rangers, Celtic or Hibernian and it was almost unheard of for a lad to be chosen from a tiny club such as Clydebank Strollers. At the time I was working on a milk round in the morning, which meant getting up at three, delivering the milk and then going back to bed for a couple of hours before getting up again and setting off for school. I can remember the morning after being selected for the Professional Youth team, leaving the bottle on doorsteps and then fishing out peoples papers from their letterboxes to read the sports pages which all had details of the Scottish side. What a thrill that was, to see the name A. Gray in the Scotland team, and one of the papers even mentioned how strange it was for a player from a junior side to be included with the cream of the nation's youth talent. I even thought about cutting the story out and sending it anonymously to Jim McLean at Dundee United with a thick red ink circle around my name, but reckoned someone would be watching the game, which was my big chance to prove myself.

The match was against England at Shawfield Stadium, the

home of Clyde, and what a game it turned out to be. I could not have planned it any better if I tried, as we won 3-2 in a very close match, and I scored two of the goals and made the other one. Next morning the milk around Drumchapel was late as I spent more time reading the match reports which were in all the papers. My eyes opened wide with surprise and delight when in one there was even a big black headline reading "It's a Gray Night for England".

That match and those goals were the passport to another visit to Tannadice, because Jim McLean and Dundee United had decided I was worth another chance. This time I went up after school to play in a night trial match and Willie insisted on coming with me. "Don't worry this time kid . . . I'll be there to look after you and make sure you get a fair deal," were Willie's reassuring words as we set off for Tannadice. I felt much easier this time with Willie alongside and more confident as well. It could not possibly be worse than the first trial and having done so well in the professional youth side, I knew I was capable of proving myself.

The trial game at Tannadice was a complete success. I scored a goal and ran myself into the ground and this time was disappointed to hear the whistle I was enjoying myself so much. After the match Jim McLean wanted a word with me in his office, and Willie as my guardian angel came along too. The manager was brief and to the point. "I think I've seen enough now. We've been watching you closely for some time and from what Maurice Friel tells me, and from what I've seen tonight, I think you've got the makings of a fair young player. I'm impressed with you and would like to sign you on schoolboy forms with a view to turning professional in the summer." I turned and looked at Willie who smiled and nodded his head. Jim McLean went on. "We'll give you a signing on fee of £20 and if and when you join us full time you can have £16 a week, of which £6 will go to pay for your digs." Well I didn't know what to do. I was bursting to say yes and sign the forms there and then before he changed his mind, but that's why Willie had come. Mum knew I would agree to absolutely anything, so my brother had been appointed as my financial adviser. I looked to

Willie for some guidance and Jim McLean, obviously seeing we were not quite sure of ourselves, left the office to give us a few minutes in private to talk things over. As soon as he left, I looked at Willie again, who was by now even more nervous than me. I swear my financial adviser was shaking with fear, and it was left to me to do the thinking and talking. Now £20 signing on fee did not seem an awful lot. I'd heard and read about lads getting ten times that from other clubs, but I wasn't going to argue the point and risk the chance of missing out altogether. "Well Willie, what do you think? . . . £20, is that O.K.? . . . is it enough?" Willie drew in a deep breath, thought for a few seconds and then came out with one of his pearls of wisdom. "It sounds all right to me. Yes . . . £10 for you and £10 for me," and that was the advice my big brother gave to me. I laugh now, because I was expecting him to conduct the negotiations and go through the contract, but in the end all he did was sit there and nod his head in agreement. When Jim McLean came back, we all shook hands, and I signed the schoolboy forms for Dundee United. I was on the first rung of the ladder and on my way at last to being a professional footballer. It was largely due to Maurice Friel, of course, who apparently had persistently pestered Jim McLean, and finally convinced him that I was worth a second bite of the cherry.

After signing for Dundee United, one or two other clubs started to sit up and show an interest, but as far as I was concerned I'd promised Jim McLean I would sign as a professional in the summer and there was no way I was going to let him down. I had to stay at school until the end of the summer term and after Easter was sitting my 'A' levels or highers as they are known in Scotland. My school work had really been neglected and had taken second place to the football by now. I took four subjects but failed them all dismally. At the time I wasn't bothered, but on reflection wish I'd spent a little more time revising. Then though, I couldn't wait to leave school and embark on my football career. Apart from my exams, the other thing that suffered was my allegiance to Rangers which died a little. It had always been the dream to run out at Ibrox in their blue number nine shirt, but Dundee United were the team that wanted me and so overnight I became one of the so-called "Tannadice Terrors".

 # DUNDEE DEBUT

It was in July 1973 that I graduated as a professional footballer. There was no tearful farewell to Glasgow because the sadness of leaving home and my Mum was matched with the excitement of starting out on the soccer trail. My Mum, of course, was upset to see me go, as any mother is when the youngest leaves, but she knew just how fortunate I'd been to land such an opportunity. She was the proudest mother in Drumchapel the day her Andrew set off for Dundee with a suitcase and a pair of boots. I was making a journey that every kid on the estate had dreamt about. All my pals over the years had shared the same ambition of playing professional football, and when I said my farewells, their goodbyes must have been tinged with some jealousy. The lads on the estate and my team mates at Clydebank Strollers were all keen to see me do well, but each and everyone would have given everything they had to be in my place. So, as I headed north for Dundee – the city of jute – I can remember feeling just how lucky I was to be getting a chance of playing football for a living. Although I was confident of doing well I didn't really have any starry-eyed hopes when I first started.

Having failed in my first trial at Tannadice, which after all was less than a year ago, I realised how wide a gap there was between juvenile or part-time non-league football and the Scottish first division. Like any other youngster starting his first job you cherish hopes that one day you'll be at the top, or achieve success, but I knew of the hundreds of teenagers who kicked off their soccer careers with Scottish clubs only a small percentage actually made it all the way. My brother James was the classic example. When he signed for Clydebank we all pulled his leg he'd be playing for Rangers one day, because there was no mistaking his skill and quality. After only two years though, he packed the game up, or rather it left him behind. For any footballer the first couple of seasons are the most demanding. At first you are filled with a natural feeling of achievement and importance, only to find that although a professional by name you are still in reality very much a triallist. Like my brother James, an awful lot of young players fail to mature or prove their potential by the time they are nineteen or twenty, and by then there is a long queue of sixteen and seventeen year-olds waiting to take their places. As in most professions where you have to either perform or entertain, it is fair to say a footballer is only as good as his last game. You can't survive for very long on reputation alone and as a striker I knew that I had to score goals to prove to myself and Dundee United that I had a football future. On the train journey north I had plenty of time to think about the coming years as I gazed through the window. It was on that very first trip I set myself a target: I was seventeen and thought or wanted to be a first-teamer by the time I was twenty one; if I couldn't make it by then, that would be the end.

Although I was still quite a shy lad, the thought of leaving home and living in digs didn't scare me as much as it should have done. Football in those early days provided me with a shield of confidence. Behind it I was self assured, but away from the game I was still quiet and at times unsure of myself. My first home in Dundee was digs in Broughty Ferry, a residential suburb of the city which is also a popular holiday resort. Dundee itself is one of Scotland's finest cities sitting proudly on the Firth of Tay. In olden days it was a thriving whaling and fishing port and owed much of its prosperity to the sea. The whalers had long gone, but the docks were still the focal point of the city's industrial life. They'd built some great ships there over the years such as the polar exploration vessels *Terra Nova* and *Discovery* and, as in many Highland cities, there were plenty of legends and lots of folklore. High above, overlooking the area, was Dundee Law which was once a volcano, and from there your eyes were caught by the giant cranes and scaffolding of the docks, the magnificent Tay bridge, the road to the south and the unmistakeable grey floodlight pylons of the two football grounds. From afar it was hard to tell which one was which. United's Tannadice Park was just across the road from Dundee's Dens Park and any football buff will tell you they are the closest grounds to each other anywhere in the British Isles.

Dundee like Glasgow was a divided city when it came to following football. Over the years the Dundee "Dark Blues" had enjoyed much better times than United. They were one of the few teams in the sixties who managed to break the Glasgow stranglehold of Rangers and Celtic and win the league championship. They had won the Scottish FA Cup and League Cup as well. By comparison, United's trophy cupboard was almost bare, with only a couple of second division championships to show in sixty years. As the older club Dundee and their followers liked to think of themselves as the senior side. Most of the city's great players had come from there as well. In the sixties they found and sold such men as that towering centre half Ian Ure, who went on to Arsenal; there was Jimmy Gabriel, a fiery wing half, who was sold to Everton; Alan Gilzean who provided so many valuable goals for Spurs; and Charlie Cook, one of the most admired and talented men to cross the border. United's most famous son in recent years had been centre half Ron Yeats who led the early Liverpool charge under Bill Shankly, whose brother Bob had ironically been manager of Dundee. When I arrived at Tannadice, United were beginning to change that tradition. Under manager Jim McLean they had established themselves in the first division and had even been acclaimed as the "Jet Set" club of the seventies. Seventeen year olds though have little time for talk of tradition and my only concern was to report to United for pre-season training.

The first day of a new season at any club is very like the first day at school. Everyone comes back from their holidays with tales to tell, there's always a smell of paint and polish, and of course a few fresh faces. One of those was mine and the first day at Tannadice was one of being shown around, issued with kit and learning a few dos and don'ts. I can vividly recall the very first training session as well. All the players joined in together and we had to race around the track on the outside of the pitch. Seeing it was the first day of training, the local paper had sent down one of its photographers to get a snap of the players for that night's back page. At the time we were running and then jumping in the air as though to head a ball and as we ran towards the camera I was at the back, with most of the first teamers at the front. I watched the photographer carefully focus his camera and just as he was about to take the picture I timed my jump into the air. It worked a treat, because that night there I was in the picture and once again the old Gray determination to get on and get noticed had struck. Although I considered myself to be fit, the training was still hard. It was so intensive it left me exhausted at the start, but how marvellous it was to be out running and playing football and actually getting paid for it. I settled down well at both the club which had a friendly atmosphere, and at the digs which I was lucky to be sharing with another youngster from Tannadice, Alan Forsyth. We trained in the week and went home to Glasgow at weekends when I'd have to give a full report to my Mum.

The Scottish soccer season always kicks off early with the opening rounds of the league cup, and after the initial fitness training Jim McLean split the squad in two. I was with the reserves, of course, and in August played my first matches in the tangerine shirt of Dundee United. There were a couple of reserve matches and a bruising encounter with an army side. I came through them all quite well and, although I failed to score, was nevertheless pleased with my own performances. In the meantime the first team had kicked off with a 2-1 league cup win at East Fife but were then held to goalless draw by Aberdeen at Tannadice. Following that match Jim McLean had some words of inspiration for all the reserves. He told us he would be watching our next reserve match against Aberdeen very closely, and a first team place was always available for anyone who could impress him enough.

We won that match at Pittodrie and although I missed out on scoring yet again, I still felt I'd had a good game. When I went to Tannadice on the Friday morning I'd forgotten all about Jim McLean's offer of a first team place, but no sooner had I walked through the door then I was told to train with the first team. After only a few weeks I could hardly believe my luck and at lunchtime was on the phone to Mum to break the incredible news . . . I'd been chosen as one of the substitutes for Saturday's league cup game against Motherwell. The opening rounds of the cup were played on a league basis and United really needed a win to qualify for the next stage.

Being with the first team that Saturday was quite an occasion and there were around 5,000 people at Motherwell's Fir Park ground to see the game. Motherwell, who were managed then by one of Scotland's great centre forwards, Ian St. John, were a decent side and had put five goals past East Fife in their last match. Running out with United, even as one of the substitutes, was a wonderful experience and I wished I could have stopped on the pitch after the pre-match kick-in instead of taking a seat on the touchline bench. The match went Motherwell's way and with some twenty minutes to go they were cruising to a 4-0 victory. I was happy sitting on the bench, watching the match, taking in the atmosphere and listening to some of Jim McLean's comments and orders as he beckoned United to get back into the game. Suddenly he turned to me, knocked me on the shoulder and said "Get stripped off and warmed up Andy . . . I want to give you a run out." For a moment I froze in my seat. This was the chance I was waiting for but suddenly an unexplainable feeling of fear had gripped me. At first I did not want to go and my legs shook as I tried to pull my tracksuit off over my boots. I can remember Jim McLean shooting a glance in my direction as if to ask what was taking me so long. Finally I was ready and on I went.

There was no fairytale start; by then we were a beaten team and all I can remember is chasing a few long balls and having a shot at goal which was so slow it would still be rolling today if the Motherwell keeper had not come off his line to pick it up. But when the whistle went and we ran towards the dressing room Jim McLean managed to smile at me while he glared at a few others, so I thought I had not done too badly. Not well enough to be picked for the next two matches, both of which were lost. It was after the second defeat, to Motherwell again, that Jim McLean let it be known he would be making a few changes for the last league cup match, which was against East Fife at Tannadice on Wednesday night . . . just three days before the start of the division one season.

He named his team on the morning of the game and there at number eight was Andy Gray. Little did I know then, but from that day there was no looking back. To the delight of the United fans at Tannadice we demolished East Fife by five goals to two and what's more I got one of them. It was the sort of goal you dream about scoring as well, and even to this day Jim McLean reckons it was one of the best headers I've ever scored. A cross came in from some thirty or forty yards out, I ran onto the ball, and headed it just inside the area. I caught it perfectly and the ball screamed past the East Fife keeper – my first full game and the first goal. Andy Gray was off and running!

On the Saturday I was named in the team and made my professional league debut at Dumbarton, and celebrated by scoring the winning goal in a 2-1 victory. The next week we opened at home with a 2-0 victory and I got another, and all of a sudden I found myself the talk of Tannadice. On the third Saturday of the season we were off to play arch rivals Dundee across the road at Dens Park. It was my first local derby and with over twelve thousand watching we won again 1-0 to go second to Celtic in the table. It was an unbelievable start for both me and the team. Only three months before I had given myself three of four seasons to get into the first team, and yet here I was top scorer in the side chasing Celtic at the top of the Scottish first division.

My brothers Willie and Duncan, and Mum of course, came to watch some of those early matches and in October the Gray's football allegiance was split for the first time in its history when Dundee United took on the mighty Rangers at Tannadice. For that one day the Gray clan sported the black and tangerine of United rather than the royal blue of Rangers but it was the Glasgow men who won easily 3-1. I didn't score that day and the strange thing is I've never managed to get one goal against Rangers. The family reckon I never had the heart to score against them because Celtic never presented any problems, but even though my first love in football were the Ibrox men all teams were treated as the enemy when I played against them. After that Rangers match I suffered my first setback as a professional when Jim McLean dropped me for the next game at Aberdeen. He wasn't dissatisfied with me but thought as a seventeen-year-old I'd been asked to do too much too soon. I was sub though, and still managed to score when I went on in the second half, which I think proved to the manager I was big enough to hold my own.

The first few months at Tannadice really flew by and there was little time for anything else, such was my preoccupation with football. I trained twice as hard as anyone else but at first it was not from choice. Although I was now a first teamer, and being paid a first team wage as well, of £50 a week, most of my pals were the lads I shared digs with who were in the reserves. After training in the morning we would set off for lunch in town and then in the afternoon while they enjoyed themselves at the cinema or around the city I was under strict orders from Jim McLean to go back to the ground for extra training. At first I thought it was so unfair. I was having to train all day, every day, while the rest of the club had their afternoons off.

At Tannadice there would be just the manager and myself. We spent the whole afternoon practising headers and shots on goal. He would provide the crosses and through balls for me to throw myself at. Now as much as I loved my football then, the extra training was hard and at times painful, because initially I regarded it as a kind of punishment. What Jim McLean was doing of course, was giving up his own afternoon to help me become a better player. Just as you try hard for a teacher you like at school, I responded to the encouragement and advice of the United manager. He was, and is, a perfectionist. His players can always be better, and I wonder sometimes if I would have had the same success had Jim McLean not taken so much time to polish my game. Amazingly the United manager had so much confidence in me after just five months that he was predicting a World Cup call-up. It came just after Christmas when we slammed Dumbarton 6-0. I got four goals and missed a penalty and on New Years Eve I could not believe

my eyes when I saw one of the headlines. "Gray In World Form
– McLean."

The United manager disclosed that Willie Ormond, the
Scottish team chief, was planning to watch me in our next game
at St. Johnstone and McLean could have hardly given me a
better reference. "If Andy Gray continues his rate of progress I
am certain he'll make the Scottish pool for Munich. I think he's
that good," was what Jim McLean had to say. I was staggered
by his prediction and I could hardly believe that after a few
months I was being pushed for a place in the Scottish side. It
was only a year since I had been rejected at that first trial at
United but there was even more startling news to come that
Hogmanay. Another headline spread across the back page of
the *Scottish Daily Express*, "Gray – Now Everton Move In"
started speculation that I could be on the move for the breathtaking sum of £150,000. Everton, Spurs, Leeds, Liverpool,
Rangers and Newcastle United, whose manager Joe Harvey
had already been involved in talks with McLean, were all
interested, it seemed, in signing me. The clubs were also
planning to watch me at St. Johnstone and I could hardly
believe it was all happening to me. A transfer was the furthest
thing from my mind and United did not want to sell me,
although even in those days the economics were more important
than anything else. We drew 1-1 with St. Johnstone and it was
not one of my better games. I never heard any more about that
Scotland call-up, and Jim McLean told me to forget about the
transfer talk. For an eighteen-year-old recruit those fees were
unreal. I was still serving my apprenticeship, having signed on
for a mere £20 and now big name clubs such as Everton, Spurs
and Liverpool were thinking of spending £150,000 on me.

My new found fame did not last long because within days I
was facing the first real crisis of my career. We were playing in a
practice match one morning and as I went into a challenge with
my roommate Alan Forsyth, of all people, I felt my right knee
give way. Never having had an injury before I didn't know what
was wrong or what to do. The physio and the club doctor had
me on the treatment bench and decided between them I needed
a cartilage operation. The very mention of the word cartilage or

ligament sets a footballer's teeth on edge. In those days the operation was one feared by every footballer. It was before the development of micro-surgery and for a cartilage operation the surgeon had to make a five or six inch incision around the knee and then literaly lift up the knee cap like a top on a tin can and delve inside to find the fault. These days, of course, with modern medicine what it is, only a small incision is needed and the cartilage operation is looked upon as purely routine. When I was facing my operation though, it was far from being a formality. Cartilage problems had finished more footballers, both young and old, than anything else and as I went into hospital I must admit I feared for the future. The surgeon and the nurses did a good job of convincing me it was all very straightforward and within three weeks of the operation I was back at Tannadice training again. At first I could only manage to hobble along the pitch but was not allowed to ease up for one minute. Jim McLean was desperate to get me fit again as the team had lost three matches in a row and the Scottish Cup competition was also on. For a couple of weeks he made my life an absolute misery. It was like being in the army with one of those belligerant sergeant majors barking orders at you. "Come on Andy, you can run faster than that. Put some more effort into it – come on lad, try, try harder," were the words from the United coaching staff which echoed around my head as I fought my way back to fitness.

The crunch came at the beginning of March when United reached the quarter finals of the cup against Dunfermline Athletic. On the Monday before the match Jim McLean called me aside after training and asked me if I thought I'd be fit to play: "You see Andy, with you in the team we've got a great chance of beating them and making the semi-finals. If they see you are back in the team after injury, it might give them too much to think about," was how the United manager saw things. Well, that week I trained harder than ever, and was even told off for limping on the Thursday when a couple of press reporters watched us training. "What do you think you're doing limping like that – you don't want to let people see that," said Jim McLean. "I can't help it," I said. "My knee is still sore and it hurts when I put too much weight on it." The quarter final with Dunfermline meant a lot to the manager and the club. Dundee had reached the last eight as well, and for the sake of local pride we could not afford to let them go through without us. On the day before the game the manager told me he was putting me in the side even if I was not one hundred per cent fit. It was the first time such a thing had happened to me but it was really a taste of the future. Jim McLean explained his decision by saying, "I reckon your name on the team sheet could be worth a goal to us Andy. Just start the game, you can come off later if your knee is troubling you." Well as it happend the manager had the game completely weighed up. He was right. It was worth a goal, mind you I didn't score it, and I had to come off towards the end because of my knee. But United were happy with a one-all draw and a replay at Tannadice. We won that 4-0 and in my first season as a professional I found myself on the verge of a cup final. In the semi-final were were up against Hearts and by the time the match came round my knee was strong again and I was fully fit.

Both semi-finals were played at Hampden Park. In the first, Celtic beat Dundee 1-0 and then three days later we drew 1-1 with Hearts. Back we went to Hampden three days later and blasted our way through 4-2. The third goal was mine and I don't think I've ever scored a sweeter one at Hampden. It was a half volley from twenty yards out and I caught it perfectly to crack it home. At the end of that match, even Jim McLean, one of the quietest and most unassuming managers on the circuit, was carried away. It was the only time I ever saw him get emotional, as he punched the air with his fist and then ran onto the pitch to congratulate the players.

As the league season petered out we had to wait until May for the final against Celtic at Hampden Park when all the eyes of Scotland were upon us. Celtic, the old enemy, were going for the double again and on a warm May Saturday with summer in the air just over 76,000 fans poured through the Hampden turnstiles. The fact that most were wearing green and white did not really matter to us because when we emerged from the dressing room side by side the roar, no matter for whom, was both deafening and warming. No game can match a cup final for atmosphere. Vital league matches, derby games, even internationals are, of course, all great occasions, but on cup final day whether it be at Hampden Park or Wembley Stadium you are filled with a sudden sense of destiny.

For some reason I had been ordered to play out on the left in the first half. Jim McLean thought it might provide Celtic with some problems, but sadly the plan backfired. We were two down at half-time with Kenny Dalglish, Dixie Deans, Jimmy Johnstone and Billy McNeil all at full throttle. At the start of the second half I was told to go out and play my normal striking role and so nearly scored with a header from six yards – I've never managed to work out how Connaghan in the Celtic goal managed to save it. In the end we went down 3-0 and watching Billy McNeil go and lift the cup was a wretched experience. Losing a cup final is something you wouldn't wish on your worst enemy. For weeks you look forward to it, and prepare for it, and get taken along with the excitement and interest it generates in the club and around the city, and then suddenly it's all over – you may just as well have got knocked out in the first round. I went back to the Hampden dressing room in tears that afternoon and was so bitterly disappointed with my losers medal I threw it into the corner. That night we went off to the club's cup final dinner, which for the players was more like a wake, and it was not until midnight that I got my medal back. To be honest I'd forgotten all about it but one of the club's officials had been clearing up in the dressing room and found the discarded medal. That night he had been checking with all the players and was relieved to discover it was mine. I took it off him so as not to hurt his feelings but vowed that next time only a winner's medal would do.

My disappointment at losing a final lasted only a few days. It had been a better season than I could have hoped for. I was United's top scorer with eighteen goals in only twenty-seven games and there were just five players in the first division who had bettered that record. What I didn't expect though was to find myself in the middle of a dressing room mutiny at Tannadice. It happened when I reported for training one day and the players got talking about new contracts and terms for the next season. At the time I was being paid £50 a week in the season which dropped to £44 in the summer. As an eighteen-year-old I was grateful to be playing football and the money was neither here nor there. The senior pros though were far from happy with the club's new offer and decided I could do them a favour. They reckoned I was the club's most valuable player. I'd been voted player of the year by the supporters' club as well, and if I were to reject the new wages offered by United, it might cause the club to think again. "Look Andy," they said. "United cannot afford to lose you. If you go and see the boss and tell him you're not going to sign unless he ups the first team money, we could all get a raise and do very nicely." That talk really frightened me, and there was no way I was going to fight other players' battles. "You must think I'm crazy. I daren't say that to the boss he might get angry with me." I may have scored a few goals and earned myself a reputation as one of the club's most promising young players, but I was still not the most confident of lads and feared having any trouble with the manager. Finally the time came when I had to go and see Jim McLean and as I left the dressing room the rest of the team looked at me and pleaded once again for me to hold out for more money.

I'm afraid I was a disappointment to them. My contract was up for renewal and the manager got the shock of his life when we started discussing terms because I think he was half expecting me to ask for a rise. "Look boss have you got a new contract for me?" I asked. Jim McLean pulled one out from a folder on his desk. "Yes it's here Andy. I've not filled in any figures yet because I thought you might want to have a chat about money and so on." "If you give me the contract now boss, I'll sign it and leave you to fill in the blank spaces." Jim McLean must have thought he was hearing things. "You mean you'll sign just like that?" "Just like that," I said. "I'm happy here and I'm enjoying my football," and with that signed my new contract. I didn't even wait to hear what the new terms were. It could have been a drop for all I knew, but Jim McLean was not a man to let anyone down and I can still picture the look of bewilderment on his face as I left his office that day having signed a blank contract. When I got back to the dressing room, the other players were desperate to find out what had been said or agreed. I told them the truth and they laughed. "You feeling all right Andy?" one said. They thought me mad of course. How could anyone sign a blank contract they asked? Well, at the time I was single, had no mortgage to pay or bills to worry about and all I wanted to do was to play football . . . for buttons if need be.

The start of the new season was totally different from the first when I'd arrived at Tannadice as a newcomer. Now I was a marked man, and all the United fans looked to me to score goals. We had a good team for the kick-off with players like Davie Narey, Ian McDonald, George Fleming, Dougie Smith and Jacky Copland all regulars. Later on Paul Sturrock and Paul Hegarty joined the squad and 1973-74 was one of the best seasons for many a year. United were rarely out of the top four and won a place in Europe. As for me, I was called into the Scotland under-23 side and became one of the few players to have turned out for the country at five levels: schoolboy, amateur youth, professional youth, juvenile and now under-23. My goalscoring was as sharp as ever and I finished that season with twenty-six goals in forty-two matches, but I nearly didn't make it to the end.

Midway through the season Nottingham Forest came in with a bid of £75,000 for me. It was turned down flat at the time, but I was told later that had the Forest manager Allan Brown increased it to £100,000 I'd have been on my way to Sherwood Forest. But after finishing up as United's player of the year for the second season running and topping the goalscorers in the first division, it seemed that sooner or later another club would come up with an offer. As always Jim McLean was scrupulously fair with me. He knew sooner or later the club would be forced to cash in. Attendances were not as good as they should have been, and like most Scottish sides United could not afford to turn away the big money offered by English clubs. As for me, I was happy whatever the outcome. I was still only nineteen and enjoying every single minute. Away from the club I was happily settled in digs with the delightful Mrs McAlman, whose home was just off the city centre. I'd had about four or five landladies in the first eighteen months but my enthusiasm proved a little too much for them. But in Mrs McAlman I met my match. She was like a mother to me and made sure I behaved myself. We had a wonderful relationship, so much so that to this very day the name of Andy Gray is held up to all the young football apprentices who arrive on her doorstep. "If you're half as good and clean and tidy as Andy Gray then you'll go far," is the way she's been greeting lads ever since. I know for a fact a few of the lads are sick and tired of hearing my name, but I can assure them I was not quite the saint everyone reckoned me to be.

One of the worst scrapes I've ever got into came while I was stopping with Mrs McAlman. It was on a Wednesday night and a few of us from the club were out enjoying ourselves in Dundee. We finished up in a local nightclub and after a couple of drinks I went off to the gents and was washing my hands and face in the basin when I was attacked. I felt a fist come crunching into my face and was so surprised and dazed by the attack that I fell back onto the floor, but just managed to catch sight of a group of blokes making for the door. Staggering back into the club with blood gushing from my forehead the local bouncers rushed to help me. When I told them what had happened they spotted the troublemakers who were a group of rival Dundee fans and once again fists started flying. I stayed out of it and later had to go to hospital to have stitches put in the cut around my eye. Jim McLean took me home to Mrs McAlman's and you can imagine the stick I got the next day when I walked into the dressing room with a real shiner. Luckily the truth about how I got my black eye never came out and just as well because the press could have gone to town on the story of Dundee fans attacking a Dundee United player in a nightclub. Mrs McAlman was most sympathetic, of course, and that week I was treated even better than usual. Another funny story about my lovely landlady is that after I left she would never let anyone have my room until she thought they deserved it. It was just as though they had to earn the Andy Gray award!

I was back with Mrs McAlman for another season in July 1975 but everyone at Tannadice knew I would not be with them much longer. Speculation about my future was the talk of the

Scottish scene, but as ever I buckled down to the pre-season training. It wasn't the best of kick-offs for me, with only two goals coming in the opening ten matches, and I was so disappointed with my own form that when manager Jim McLean was bad tempered one Friday morning in training, I thought he was going to drop me. Sure enough I didn't play against Celtic on the Saturday . . . I was 300 miles away south of the border, in England starting out on the next chapter of my soccer story.

5 A PASSAGE TO ENGLAND

They always say a week in politics is a long time, but the most hectic seven days of my life would have taken some beating. It started with me nearly being shipped off to a new career in Germany, and finished with me signing for Aston Villa in a record £110,000 deal.

The chance to go to the continent came completely out of the blue because at the time foreign deals were virtually unheard of. In the early sixties John Charles, Denis Law, Joe Baker, Jimmy Greaves and Gerry Hitchens had all courted the Italian clubs without a great deal of success. And in Europe there had been a lot of movement but no British players had been tempted to leave these shores. So, when I found myself at the centre of a sensational bid of £150,000 from the German side Schalke 04, history could have been in the making. This was two years before Kevin Keegan took off to play for Hamburg and he was followed, of course, by Tony Woodcock who went to Cologne and Dave Watson who had a brief spell with Werder Bremen. At the time though I didn't realise the significance of becoming the first British player for some years to attract the attention of foreign football. It all started on my return from a UEFA Cup match in Iceland with Dundee United when there was a strange message waiting for me at the digs. A Mr Neef had been trying to contact me and would be calling back later. It turned out to be Gerry Neef, the former Rangers goalkeeper, who was doing some work and scouting for the German side Schalke 04. On his recommendation they were interested in signing me and were prepared to bid up to £150,000.

I knew Dundee United would jump at such an offer and

suddenly my life was sent spinning. Over the past few weeks I'd thought a lot about my future and was hoping that a transfer would take me to either Rangers or one of the top English clubs who had been tailing me since last season. I knew nothing of Schalke but agreed to meet Gerry Neef in order to learn more. At our first meeting, the chance to live abroad and play in the land of the Beckanbauers and Mullers seemed most attractive, and the sort of terms Gerry Neef mentioned could only be described as out of this world. He was talking thousands with a life of luxury thrown in as well. I couldn't help but be interested and so a secret meeting was set up for a Sunday night. It was agreed that I would meet Gerry Neef along with Schalke's manager and coach at the Albany Hotel in Glasgow. I was injured that week and so missed United's match against Motherwell which was really a blessing in disguise. With so much on my mind I could hardly think straight and was hardly in the right mood, or shape, for a game of football.

On the Sunday I travelled down to Glasgow and met up with my financial adviser, big brother Willie of course, who had agreed to come along. Remembering the last time we'd been together when I signed on at Tannadice Park for £20, Willie promised me on this occasion he'd make sure I'd get a better deal. It was hard to imagine that less than two years ago we'd been sitting in Jim McLean's office talking about £16 a week, and yet here we were, in our best suits on the way to one of Glasgow's swishest hotels, with a cheque for £150,000 in the offing. The meeting had been fixed for Sunday evening to give the German officials time to fly over, and Gerry Neef was keen we should meet under cover of darkness in case the story leaked out. They were well aware that other clubs were chasing me, and hoped to be the early birds and clinch a deal swiftly before other sides had a chance to prepare their offers. So, after Sunday tea at Mum's, Willie and I set off for our clandestine meeting. I swear sometimes that football directors and managers would make good secret agents, as the lengths some go to when they try to sign players never cease to amaze me. I've heard of managers putting on a disguise to go and watch players so nobody knows they're interested. There have been meetings in motorway cafes, lonely lay-bys and remote hotels and when reporters have got onto the scent of a big deal there have even been car chases. And the Schalke talks were a real cloak and dagger affair, but very exciting. "How will they know us Andy?" Willie asked. "I know Gerry Neef and presumably he'll be waiting for us at the hotel or he'll be up in his room," I replied. It was questions from Willie like that which got the butterflies going, and as we got nearer to the Albany Hotel the worse they got. I didn't speak a word of German and was relying on Mr Neef to do most of the talking.

Finally we got there, and as we walked through the door I spotted Gerry Neef who was standing at the reception desk. He jumped to attention and started waving and running towards us, but did not look at all happy. In fact he looked angry and his face was white with fear. Instead of greeting us with a handshake, he grabbed hold of both Willie and I and bustled us back through the doors and out on to the pavement. At that moment a car pulled up, the door sprung open and he pushed us into the back seat and then jumped in alongside. For a moment I wondered what on earth was going on. It was like a scene from *The Godfather*, especially with a strange dark figure sitting in the front seat. Now, although I was hoping for one of those offers you can't refuse, I was hardly expecting a cops and robbers car drive through the streets of Glasgow. As soon as Gerry got his breath back he explained his unusual behaviour. Apparently ten minutes before we were due to arrive Dixie Deans, the Celtic centre forward, had shown up at the hotel with some friends to have a night out and was sitting in the foyer. Fearing that Dixie would recognise me, and perhaps blow the secret of this hush-hush transfer, Gerry had been pacing up and down waiting for our arrival, his main problem being there was more than one way into the Albany and he simply did not know which way we were coming. So, the start of my meeting with Schalke had hardly got off to a great start, but our problems were far from over. The German delegation, having flown in that afternoon, had not had the chance to eat and were ravenously hungry. We all agreed to find a restaurant where we could eat and talk the deal over. Off we went on a magical mystery tour of Glasgow's eating houses. Late on a Sunday night is not the best time to eat in any British city and we could not find a single restaurant open anywhere. We tried all the ones we knew, and Gerry Neef knew, and I was just beginning to imagine us in some down town chippy or burger bar, talking over a tomato sauce bottle, when we spotted a little Italian restaurant with the lights still on. Gerry jumped out and went into the restaurant and re-appeared seconds later with the Italian owner. In typical fashion he was waving his arms in the air as Gerry stood pleading with him to let us in. It was nearly ten o'clock by now. The restaurant was empty, all the tables had been washed and cleared and the owner was ready for his bed. Finally he agreed to let us in, and so the transfer talks finally got underway.

The Schalke offer was an amazing one. Their manager was talking in telephone numbers and both Willie and I listened in astonishment as they outlined a package which would have made me one of the highest paid teenagers in the world. They were prepared to give me a signing on fee of £100,000 and a contract worth between £60,000 and £70,000 a year. They seemed pleasant and genuine enough men as well, who were anxious to introduce some British talent into their team. But if anything their offer was too good to be true for me and that's why Willie and I left the restaurant that night with the deal still on the table. I didn't doubt for a minute that Schalke would have honoured every agreement and kept all their promises, but what is it about human nature that makes you suspicious when such a lucky break comes along? I kept asking myself, why me, why should a German side want to buy me so badly? What was the catch?

There wasn't one, of course, other than the risk of moving to a foreign country and leaving your family and friends behind. I turned Schalke down for two reasons. The first was that I had always planned or hoped to try my luck in English soccer. And secondly, I was frightened of moving to the continent. Apart from football trips I'd never lived more than 100 miles from home and the thought of being stuck in a lonely flat in Germany terrified me. Not being able to speak the language or communicate with anyone I wouldn't have been able to pick up the phone to see if my mates fancied going out for a quick drink. If Schalke had another British player on the books I might have given the move a little more thought, but at nineteen I didn't fancy being a lone ranger. The money, mind boggling as it was, never really came into it. More important then was my life and my football career. Had the offer come three or four years later I would have jumped at the chance, but there's many a player who has gone abroad with hopes of riches and fame, only to discover there's no place like home.

For the rest of the week I cross-examined myself time and time again over whether I had done the right thing. What if another club did not come in with a bid; what if I was dropped from the Dundee United side; no one would be interested then. And I was convinced after training on Friday morning that Jim McLean was going to leave me out of the team for the match against Celtic. He always drove me hard in training and shouted his orders out, but this morning there was a coldness in both his manner and voice. He was most unfriendly and never stopped moaning – I just couldn't do anything right. After changing, I was on my way out of the door when Jim McLean's voice boomed at me from down the corridor. "Where can I get in touch with you this afternoon?" said the manager, in a very terse manner. His question surprised me for a moment, because he knew full well if United were playing a match in Glasgow I travelled ahead on the Friday to stop the night at my Mum's in Drumchapel before meeting up with the rest of the players the next day. So I snapped back at him, "I'll be at my Mum's where else?" and off I stormed, slamming the door behind me. It was about the closest I ever came in two years to having an argument with Jim McLean, so good was our relationship. I got a lift back to Glasgow after training with my United teammate Jacky Copland, and as we pulled out of Tannadice I can remember telling him I was going to be dropped from the team. "Did the boss say he was going to drop you Andy? . . . He wouldn't dare leave you out at Celtic," said Jacky. "But he wanted to know where I was going to be this afternoon, so perhaps he's going to pick his team and then break the news that I'm being left out by phone rather than face me with it," I reasoned.

I really should have known the United manager better, because he was one of the fairest and kindest I've ever played for. When we got to Glasgow I made for my girlfriend's house, which was just down the road from my Mum's. I'd just sat down with a cup of tea when the phone went . . . it was my Mum. "Andy, I've just had United on the phone, you've got to ring Tannadice as soon as possible. It's very important," she said. Instead of dialling Dundee straight away, I finished my tea and then summoned up the courage to ring Jim McLean. I was convinced I was being dropped, and once again his manner was sharp. "You can forget about playing at Celtic tomorrow Andy," was his opening attack. Then he paused, and I started to go cold. Jim McLean went on "The fact is, we've agreed terms with Aston Villa for you and the deal has got to go through tonight – they want to meet you down there this evening. If you get your skates on there's a flight from Glasgow and you'll just about make it in time. Shall I ring and tell them you're on the way?" For a moment I nearly said no. It had all come so quickly and I needed time to gather my thoughts. I knew of Aston Villa of course, but to be honest hadn't a clue where they played. "Well," said Jim McLean. "Shall I ring them Andy and say you'll meet them? I think it would be a good thing for you." This time Jim sounded gentler – more like his old self. He had always promised he would sell me to a good club when the time came, and so I thought if Jim was in favour of it, then I should go and see Aston Villa. "Yes I've got to pack my bag and things and then I'll be off as quick as I can," I told the United manager. Then I sprinted round to my Mum's house in Lillyburn Place and broke the news to her. She was excited of course, but before I left I needed to know one thing. Where on earth was Aston Villa?

It was a football name I'd know since I was a boy and they'd been in the news only last season having won promotion to the English first division. We got a map out and scanned the Midlands, finally deciding that it must be somewhere near Birmingham since I was due to meet their manager Ron Saunders at the city's Elmdon Airport. I packed a weekend bag, promised to let my Mum know what was happening and

I always have enjoyed scoring goals and always will.

ABOVE *My first winners' medal at Lochgoin Primary; 1-0 and Glasgow Champions. I got the goal.*

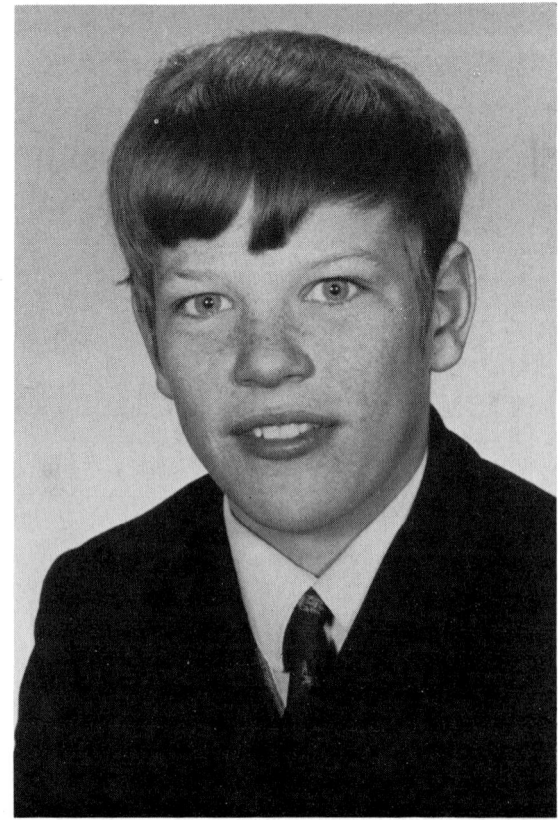

RIGHT *Aged 13 and too small to be taken seriously.*

ABOVE *My own beautiful family: Janet and our wonderful Amy.*

LEFT *The Gray clan:* back *myself and Duncan;* front *William, Mum and James.*

RIGHT *Dundee United v Celtic,
Scottish Cup Final. Got
hammered 3-0.*

ABOVE LEFT *One of my greatest mates, Alex Cropley celebrating a goal with yours truly.*

ABOVE RIGHT *A familiar sight at Villa Park: a Gray goal and huge crowds.*

BOB THOMAS

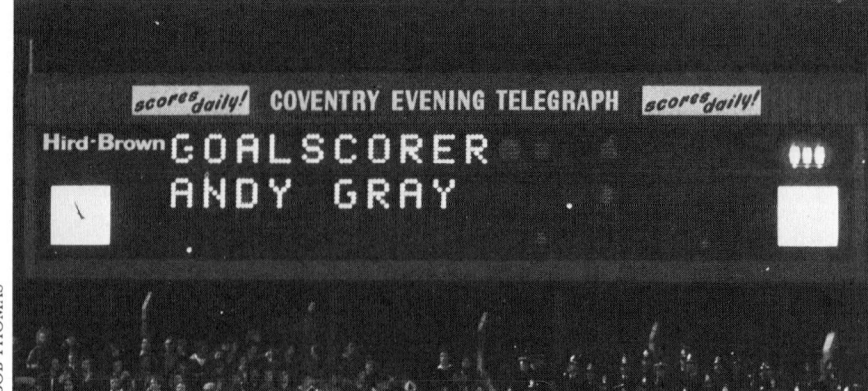

ABOVE *I knew my name would be in lights one day.*

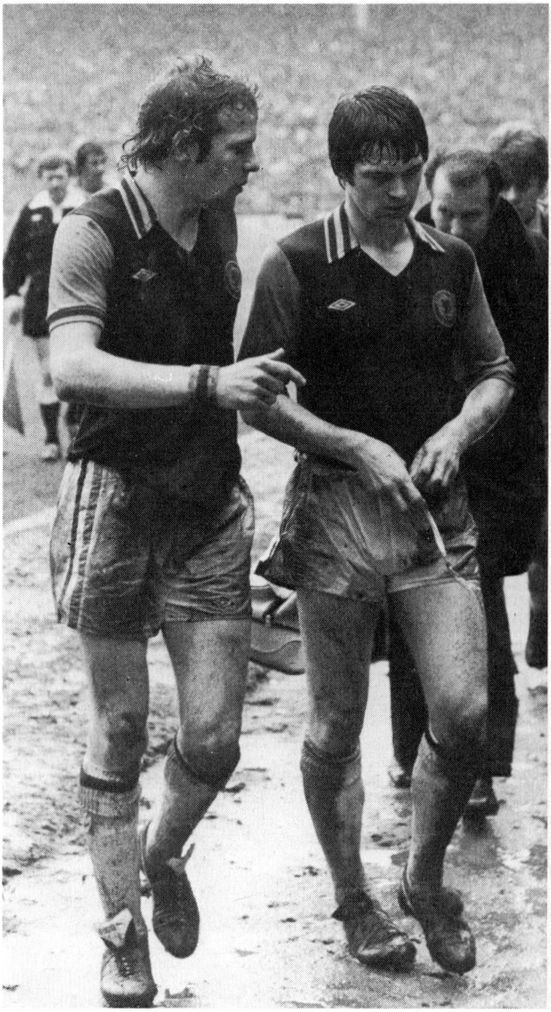

RIGHT *The man who did more than anyone to create my early success – the brilliantly talented Brian Little.*

ABOVE *One of my easier headed goals in a 4-0 win over West Ham.*

LEFT *My most prized possessions: the Players' Player and Young Player of the Year Awards won in the same year, 1976-77.*

BOB THOMAS

BOB THOMAS

ABOVE *Back home in Glasgow with the kids where I used to play at their age.*

BELOW *Behind the bar at my disastrous nightclub venture.*

jumped in a taxi bound for Glasgow airport. With only minutes to spare I made it to the Birmingham plane and off we went. Landing at Elmdon I wandered through the check-in area to be met by Aston Villa's manager Ron Saunders and the club's scout Neville Briggs, who had been watching me in Scotland. While Mr Saunders and I shook hands I could see Neville looking me up and down with a puzzled expression. "You're bigger than I thought Andy," he said. At the time I didn't take much notice of his remark and brushed it aside. It was only later the truth dawned, and the joke I'm afraid was on me. I was around 5 feet 10 inches tall but at that time the latest fashion were high-heeled boots with thick raised soles and of course, the only shoes I'd taken to Birmingham in the rush were the ones I was wearing, the platform boots, which made me look about six feet two or three. Apparently the word went round that Aston Villa were signing a giant of a Scottish centre forward and I can still hear the laughter of the other players when they discovered the truth – I was a good four inches smaller in my socks.

Villa took me to a local hotel on the Friday night and the deal was fairly straightforward. The fee was around £110,000, a record for both Dundee United and Aston Villa, at the time. I found Ron Saunders a firm and straight man who clearly had ambitions for his team and went about achieving them in a very dedicated and professional manner. Later, I discovered another side to the man, and in the end he was the main reason I left the club. For the first couple of seasons though, we got on well enough with each other. There were two intriguing stories behind my transfer to Villa. The first was that Ron Saunders, who proudly boasts how he snapped me up for a bargain price from the backwaters of Dundee, and then sold me four years later for £1.4m, had never actually seen me play before I joined Villa. His scouts had apparently been following my progress along with a few other managers but Mr Saunders had never been to watch me himself. The second, he probably got me for a knock down fee. United were really hoping for around £150,000, but at the time there were rumours about players being given freedom of contract. Jim McLean told me a few years later that, at first he wasn't keen to let me go to Aston Villa, but had been persuaded when Ron Saunders worried him with the freedom of contract talk. He made Jim think that if the rules about contracts changed I would be a free agent when my agreement ran out at the end of the season, and United would be better off getting money for me while they could. It was clever negotiating on Ron Saunders' part, I suppose, because with his team back in division one he was busily rebuilding his side.

I signed for him on the Saturday; only four days before he'd paid out another £100,000 for Blackpool goalkeeper John Burridge, who was the first Villa player I met in Birmingham. We were both staying in the same hotel at Sutton Coldfield and, as Ron Saunders left me there on the first Friday night, he said he would introduce me to another of his lads. Across the bar bounced Budgie Burridge, who looked more like a gardener than a top footballer. He was wearing a grubby old T-shirt and the tattiest pair of jeans which were held together by patches. With a smile that covered his face and a handshake that just about took your arm off Budgie made me feel at home straight away, and we've been the best of mates ever since.

Budgie, for me, is the most amazing character I've ever met in football. We were together at Villa for a couple of seasons and then our paths crossed again at Wolves. He's never changed and whenever I need cheering up a phone call to Budgie is the best tonic. He is, in his way, a legendary figure in football. There can't be a dressing room in the country that has not got its favourite John Burridge story. He's the Norman Wisdom of football if you like, who's always got a crack or a trick up his sleeve. Budgie, I reckon, could make a good living for himself as a stand-up comedian when he retires, but for all his laughs, the guy on his day is a great goalkeeper and I've yet to meet a more dedicated professional. I thought I loved my football until I met Budgie who, if possible would play or train all day every day. They used to joke at Wolves that if you phoned Budgie up at two in the morning and told him to get to the ground for early morning training under the floodlights, he'd be there. His wife Janet tells another story of Budgie's devotion to football with the tale of one of their nights out.

One afternoon he phoned up home to ask Janet if she'd like to go out for a special night and have a bite to eat as well. She got changed and did her hair and when Budgie arrived home Janet was at her glamourous best. So as not to spoil the surprise she didn't ask John where they were going, but soon wished she had. They were off to a football match, and even worse to stand on the terraces in the freezing cold behind the goal. Budgie wanted to watch Peter Shilton in action from close range, so they stood behind his goal, had a cup of soup at half-time, before switching ends to watch the England keeper in the second half. On the way home they called in for fish and chips – that was Budgie's idea of a special night out!

Whichever club he went to he was, of course, the dressing room joker. On one foreign trip abroad with Aston Villa Budgie set himself up as a customs officer and stopped all the passengers as they got in to the airport building. He inspected all the passports, searched a few cases and even confiscated someone's duty free booty. When the real customs officer discovered his trick all hell was let loose, but as usual, the big Budgie grin got him out of trouble. Another time at Wolves the players decided to play a trick on Budgie, when we were all invited to a Christmas dance in the town. Some of the lads told him it was a dinner jacket do, while others informed him they were going in fancy dress. It was neither, but Budgie brought the house down when he arrived in both a dinner jacket and fancy dress. He wore half a dinner jacket, half a pair of trousers, half a clean white shirt, half a dicky bow and one brightly polished shoe; that was the right hand side. His left hand side was a tramp's tatty shirt, jacket, trousers and old boot. Not surprisingly Budgie Burridge usually had the loudest and last laugh of all. With him looking after me how could I go wrong in Birmingham in those first few months with Aston Villa.

One of the memorable parts of the transfer deal was arriving at Villa Park for the very first time. There are some grounds that lift you from the first moment you walk in, and Villa Park was one. On my first Saturday with them, September 27th, 1975, it was a local derby day, and a crowd of 53,782 packed in to watch Villa play their arch rivals – the Blues of Birmingham City. I watched from the stand that day, and to me Villa Park was like

Hampden Park on cup final day. At Tannadice our average gate had only been around the five thousand mark and what a fabulous sensation, I felt, to be involved with a team such as Aston Villa, who as Tommy Docherty once remarked, could pull a crowd by just hanging out eleven claret and blue shirts to dry.

The following Saturday I made my debut for Villa, but it was a long way from the singing stands of Villa Park, almost the opposite in fact, because Villa's next match was away to Middlesbrough at Ayresome Park, which has never been one of my favourite grounds. It's a long journey north on the coach, and the ground itself always seems cold and lifeless. The match finished in a goalless draw and was something of an anti-climax for me. In ninety minutes I had just one half chance, but that was all. My next game was far more memorable. On the Wednesday night Villa faced the mighty Manchester United in the third round of the League Cup at Villa Park. The ground was throbbing again that night with over 41,000 people there, and although we lost 2-1 I scored on my home debut for my new team.

It was that night my love affair with Villa and its supporters really started. The Holte End, a large steeply banked terrace behind one of the goals, is where the Villa faithful congregate. When I scored I automatically ran to the mass of claret and blue scarves and threw myself in the air. It was love at first sight. From that night on I adored playing for the Villa fans who in return enjoyed my success with me. Referees these days are trying to stop players running and celebrating in front of spectators, but to me it's a vital part of the game. I know one of the most learned football directors of our time, anthropologist Desmond Morris, went to great lengths to annalyse why players celebrate as they do, calling it, "a frenzied outburst of abandoned leaping and embracing. A peak moment of tribal life enjoyed to the full with all physical barriers down and all the usual inhibitions swept away." People outside the game think we overdo it, but to me there is no greater satisfaction or enjoyment than seeing the looks of sheer joy and celebration on the faces of fans. They are the ones we play for and, for many, their whole lives revolve around the success or failure of a football team. When you play for, or support a team, you are part of that club together. The fans are just as important, and they should be allowed to enjoy success with you. That's perhaps why I had such a wonderful rapport with the Holte Enders, and have always been popular with crowds. I've always enjoyed my football and like to show it when I score a goal. The fans, I think, appreciate it and are rewarded by knowing that your heart is with theirs. Not all players think the same. I can remember telling one of Villa's younger players, Gary Shaw, to celebrate more after scoring, as he usually let his arms drop by his side and then turned and ran back up the field. "You're not being fair to the fans," I told him. "They look forward to a match all week. They come to be entertained and it's our job to give them what they want and send them home happy." I think he took notice of the advice. As for me I had quite a lot of celebrating to do in those first few weeks with Villa.

My home League debut against Spurs finished in a 1-1 draw and I scored again. A few weeks later I was back up in Scotland to play for the national under-23 side. It was a game against Denmark at Hearts' Tynecastle Park ground and I finished up with a hat-trick in a 4-1 win. After that match the Scottish papers were calling me the new Denis Law and reckoned it was only a question of time before I won my first full cap. Being compared to such a player as Denis Law was indeed a great honour. He was an idol of every lad of my age, but I was a completely different player to him. Law was a drifter who had the rare knack of being in the right place at the right time and pounced at goal like a hawk on its prey. I was a more robust player, far more aggressive than Denis, and would run twice as far and twice as fast during a match. Hopefully though, I could be as successful as the legendary Law when it came to scoring goals.

In December my promotion to the Scotland team was announced, and on a raw winter's night I played in the number nine shirt alongside Kenny Dalglish against Romania at Hampden. The last few months had been very kind to me: a record transfer to the English first division, where I was hitting the headlines; a hat-trick for the under-23 side; and now the finishing touch, a Scottish cap. Whether it all came too soon I don't know, but I played a real stinker in my first international and learnt one valuable lesson, not to believe your own publicity! On both sides of the border I was being hailed as the new Greaves, Law or by older statesman as another Lawton or Bould, but playing for Scotland that first time I realised at only twenty I still had an awful lot to learn.

After Christmas I got my head down at Villa, worked away at my game whilst trying to forget or ignore the publicity and attention which kept coming my way. I ended up with ten goals from thirty League games which wasn't too bad for my first taste of English football. The Villa team, remembering it was their return season in the top division, had pulled through fairly well finishing just below half way in the table. A club record fee of £175,000 had been spent on signing midfield player Dennis Mortimer from Coventry and you could sense that manager Ron Saunders was gradually changing the team with the accent more on younger players. Ian Ross, Jimmy Cumbes, Charlie Aitken and Chico Hamilton – players who had helped Villa back to the top, were cast off and in their places came men like fellow Scot Gordon Smith from St. Johnstone, local boy John Deehan and another Scot Alex Cropley arrived from Arsenal. Smith and Cropley, a former Hibernian player, became firm friends and the team spirit at Villa Park was beginning to generate an exciting atmosphere. We all believed we were on the verge of an important breakthrough. For me personally the move to England had worked better than I imagined. I bought my own house, a little semi in one of the suburbs, and was adjusting to the life of a football star. Aston Villa, no matter what they were doing, were and still are, the Midlands' top team. You might have been contradicted by Derby fans back in the mid-seventies or more recently by followers of Nottingham Forest and West Bromwich Albion, but none had the charisma of Villa. It was all down to tradition I suppose. Villa had always been a big team in the Midlands. In the early years they had won six League championships and a record seven FA Cups, and had also done the League and Cup double before the turn of the century.

Although their recent record was far from a glittering one, there was still a strong following in and around the second city for the Villa. Even in their third division days a crowd of 45,567 were at Villa Park to see them winning promotion. Villa were Birmingham's most fashionable side and anyone who played for them was accorded a special place in the community. Many players and managers have failed at Villa Park because they treated the club as just an ordinary run of the mill side. Aston Villa was, and still is, something special for me and the golden year was just about to unfold.

6 THE GOLDEN YEAR

Grant me just one football wish, and I'd take myself back to August 1976 to enjoy once again the best season of my career – the Golden Year. There are two main reasons why I'd love to relive that season. First of all, for me personally, it was the most successful. With twenty-five goals in thirty-six League games I finished as top scorer in the first division and have never beaten that total since. Villa won the League Cup and then I became the only man in the history of the game to win both the Player of the Year and Young Player of the Year Awards. My second reason for going back in time would be to right two wrongs. I've very few regrets about my life, but in the middle of that golden year I committed two grave sins. I was stupidly sent off whilst playing for Scotland, which to this day I'm convinced cost me a World Cup place in Argentina and was also guilty of my one and only indiscretion in front of a football crowd.

Life then was like a rollercoaster. Each corner I turned there was something new and exciting waiting for me. Each peak I reached was more rewarding and luckily each unexpected dive was over quickly. Like all the good times in life the season went so fast, and that's another reason why I'd like to relive it again. The second time around I'd take more time to appreciate everything.

My manager at Villa Park, Ron Saunders, has said only recently that fame came too swiftly for me to handle. I dismiss that observation, because on the whole, I think I handled my life fairly well . . . or at least, as well as any twenty-one year-old would. I made a few mistakes and misjudgements on the way, but haven't we all? Looking back I coped with virtually everything thrown into my path that year, which included a day when I was asked to help fix one of football's famous ceremonies. It was a year to remember all right, and that's why I'd like to go back in time, and enjoy it once more.

Aston Villa with their new look team were rated as dark horses at the start of the 1976-77 season. Liverpool were the champions with a star studded line-up which included internationals such as Ray Clemence, Phil Neal, Emlyn Hughes, Kevin Keegan, John Toshack and Steve Heighway; they were the team to beat. Ipswich Town, under the influence of Bobby Robson, were beginning to emerge from the sleepier surroundings of Suffolk. The two Manchester clubs looked threatening as well. City with Tony Book in charge had one of the most feared front-lines in the country: Brian Kidd, Dennis Tueart, Asa Hartford and Joe Royle were four men who were capable of destroying the best. Across at Old Trafford, Dave Sexton had United back on course with exciting players such as Lou Macari, Sammy McIlroy, Steve Coppell and Gordon Hill. And then there were the other dark horses besides Villa, the Geordies Newcastle United. They were lacking in star names but made up for it with a solid, reliable and well organised team of triers.

The Villa side that kicked off the season had John Burridge in goal, John Gidman and Gordon Smith were the full-backs and Welsh international Leighton Phillips and Chris Nicholl the centre backs. Dennis Mortimer, Frank Carrodus and later Alex Cropley provided the midfield influence and up front there was Ray Graydon, Brian Little and myself. Graydon was later replaced by John Deehan and John Robson switched between midfield and defence. It was a team in every meaning of the word. Together we played well and mixed well, the one aim was to win for Aston Villa. Teamwork though, was and still is, a hallmark of Ron Saunders' management. He's never believed in star players or big names and has built quite a reputation with the way he's shaped winning sides. And his reputation was certainly riding high at the start of the 1976-77 season. He picked up the coveted Manager of the Month award as Villa proudly marched to the top of the table.

In the first match at Villa Park we hit four goals past West

Ham United as Ray Graydon and I got two apiece. We lost then to Manchester City but bounced back with a 2-0 win over Everton at Goodison and then strengthened our grip and furthered our reputation with a 5-2 victory over Ipswich Town. It was that game more than any other, I think, that heralded the arrival of Aston Villa as a true first division force and marked the acceptance of Andy Gray as a quality goalscorer.

Against Ipswich I hit my first hat-trick for Villa. All three goals came in a whirlwind twenty minute spell in the second half. And the story behind that match could easily have come from the world of "Roy of the Rovers". In the first half Ipswich were all over us and we were lucky to draw 1-1 at half-time. I was having a nightmare of a match up front and could not do anything right. I couldn't even kick the ball straight. All the shots I tried were hopelessly off target and every pass went astray. It's wrong for a craftsman to blame his tools but my new boots were the big problem. For that game I'd agreed with a football boot firm to wear their latest style and had been struggling in them since kick-off. They didn't feel right at all, and instead of getting softer and suppler as the game went on, they got stiffer, and my feet sorer. So, at half-time when several of the Villa team were wondering what was wrong with me, I took off the new boots, threw them in a corner and reached for my old ones. I've often wondered since, if it really was the boots or whether I was just using them as an excuse. Whatever the truth, the old boots made all the difference to me and the new stylish ones I'm afraid went back in the box and stayed there. In the second half Villa were transformed and we paralysed Ipswich with a surge of attacks. The first was a flying header, the second was a scorching left footer and the third a vicious volley. It was the best hat-trick I've ever scored in the first division and earned some glowing reports and comments from amongst others Ipswich manager Bobby Robson.

It was his team's first defeat of the season and afterwards he told the press, "I just can't believe it. Andy Gray knocks three goals in and we must have dropped twelve places in the table. But if this fellow Gray can keep on finishing as accurately as that, Villa can stay on top. His aggression was horrendous. He

ran and worked harder than any striker I've seen in years."
That was Bobby Robson's verdict, the last part of which has
always stayed with me because he was the first man to really put
his finger on the Gray game. I'm not the most talented centre
forward in the first division, nor the most accurate in front of
goal. What I lack in skill though, I more than make up for in
effort. Too many centre forwards are happy to wander in and
out of the game and just wait for a chance to come up.

My football philosophy is the same one as I use for life. If you
want something you have to go and get it. So, as a striker I give
everything I have in a game and try to make life hell for all the
centre halves and defences I come up against. That often means
running here, there and everywhere and throwing myself at
every half chance. If you work on a centre half and wear him
down physically and mentally sooner of later he'll slip or crack,
and then you pounce on goal. That's always been my game – a
simple one really – if you try hard and give everything you have,
sooner or later the breaks will come your way. Some people in
the past have called me careless, or too brave for my own good,
as my daredevil style has brought a few serious injuries. My
answer is I can only play the way I know best, and through the
years the goals and the trophies have more than made up for the
pain. It was my unshakeable commitment to my game and to
Aston Villa that made life so enjoyable in that golden year. The
Ipswich match set the ball rolling, and from then until Christmas
I've never had a more successful run. In twenty games I scored
eighteen goals. A purple patch if ever there was one, as Villa
challenged for the championship.

The team ticked over like a highly tuned engine. Alongside
me in the Villa attack was Brian Little, and if I could pick a
team to play in he would always be there. My partnership with
him was the best I've ever had. It was probably not the most
successful in terms of trophies, but the understanding between
us was almost telepathic. He knew exactly where, and how to
find me on the field, and without any pre-match plans or
discussion our moves and attacks would work like well drilled
raids. It was a natural partnership with Brian's intelligent
running and passing providing the perfect foil for my drive and

finishing. We scored fifty-five goals between us that season and must have been the scourge of every defence. Brian, who unluckily had to retire early because of injury, was a vastly underrated player and never earned the recognition at either international of club level which he deserved. Had it not been for my injuries at Villa Park, I think Brian and I could have achieved great things. But even so, the goals we scored that season were all worth savouring. After that Ipswich game, I was swept back home to Glasgow on the crest of a wave to play for Scotland against Finland at Hampden Park. I scored my first goals for the national team, getting two in a 6-0 victory which was being used as a warm-up for the World Cup.

Life then was a dream. Villa were charging on in the first division and Scotland were confidently planning ahead to the World Cup in Argentina. I was on top of that rollercoaster of mine, but October 13th brought the first alarming dip, and the first of my two mistakes.

Scotland were playing Czechoslovakia in Prague in the opening qualifying match for the 1978 World Cup Finals. We were drawn in group seven, with Wales the other nation looking for a ticket to South America. Scottish hopes were high, because it was virtually the same side that had hammered Finland which took the field in Prague. What a well balanced team it looked. Up front I was with Kenny Dalglish and Joe Jordan, and there was a strong contingent of anglo-scots in the team with Bruce Rioch, Don Masson and Archie Gemmill making up the midfield. The Czechs, like all Eastern European sides, were a hard, uncompromising team who posed the biggest threat to our World Cup ambitions. In Prague that night we were certainly up against it as 38,000 loyal Czech followers poured into the ground to cheer their team on. Despite being away from home, we settled down well and had the match under control in the first half. I was being marked by a giant of a centre half by the name of Anton Ondrus, who like so many of his team mates played with a stern, unfriendly look on his face. He was a hard player all right, and from the start his tackles and challenges in the air carried the force of a sledgehammer. With about five or six minutes to go to half-time it was still 0-0; a satisfying scoreline for us, but not so good for the Czechs, who were being willed on by their supporters. Suddenly when the ball was not even near me, I felt a sudden sharp blow as Ondrus rammed his elbow into my face. We were jogging side by side at the time with ball having been played behind us and Ondrus followed up by pushing me to the ground. He ran off, but without thinking, I jumped up and chased after him. I grabbed hold of Ondrus, spun him round, and delivered a powerful right hook to his face which even old Henry Cooper would have been proud of. Ondrus collapsed to the ground with his face buried in his hands and began to roll over. The punch may have stung him, but this was Ondrus the actor at work as he writhed in make-believe pain. Suddenly I could hear the blast of the referee's whistle and was bustled and jostled by some of the other Czech players. A couple of my Scottish mates came to the rescue and finally the referee managed to restore the peace. Ondrus was still only half way through his dying duck routine as the rest of the Czechs remonstrated with the referee. Although I didn't understand a word they were saying I could tell by their actions they were accusing me of attacking their centre half and demanding I be sent off.

The referee hadn't seen what had gone on, but one of the linesman had and he came on to give his blow by blow account. I could see the linesman pointing in my direction and after a few seconds the referee turned and sent both Ondrus and myself off. As I made my way off the crowd jeered and whistled, and inside I was blazing with anger for being so stupid. We'd been warned to keep out of trouble before the game, as sides like Czechoslovakia were masters at baiting players. Like a fool I had fallen for their trick and retaliated. It was one of the few moments when I've lost my head on a football field and perhaps it was the Glasgow boy inside me that had risen to the trouble. In Drumchapel nobody walked away from a fight. It was one of the commandments of life up there. If you were hit, you struck back, and that's what I had done, but how I regretted it as I made for the dressing room alone. I slammed the door behind me, threw myself on the bench and put my head in my hands in despair. A few minutes later I heard a rumble of noise from the crowd, followed by the clatter of studs as the rest of the players came off for half-time. They all came over and tried to console me, but there was no disguising the disappointment on the face of the Scottish manager Willie Ormond. I had let him, and the rest of the team down, along with the millions of Scottish fans who would be watching the game back home on television. It was the first time I've ever been sent off, and what a place and time I had chosen.

During half-time the manager went through plans of how to play with ten men and when the rest of the team got up to out for the restart I stayed where I was. I could have gone out and sat on the bench I suppose, but I hadn't the heart. For forty-five minutes I sat motionless, staring into space. Guilt dominated my thoughts; if only I had stayed down and let Ondrus get sent off on his own. Why had I retaliated? Although I could hear the crowd in the distance I didn't know what was going on and when the dressing room door finally opened the players' hanging heads told me the worst – Scotland had lost. They had lost all rhythm in the second half as Czechoslovakia had taken over to end up as 2-0 winners. I felt even worse then, of course, and started to blame myself for the defeat. When I went it was still 0-0 and a draw would have been a good result to start the World Cup campaign. Instead, we were a beaten nation and it was Andy Gray's temper that had left Scotland to fight with ten men.

At the time I couldn't leave the Scottish team quick enough, and although the sending-off severely hit my international career, it also made me a better player. I promised myself I would never get caught again, and realised then how costly a lost temper could be. In future I would fight my emotions, count to ten and walk away, so if I could go back to that night in Prague again, I'd lie there on the pitch and let Ondrus take all the blame. The sending-off cost me a lot more than damaged pride. I was banned for three internationals, a suspension which in reality ruled me out of the rest of the World Cup qualifying games and cost me about a dozen or so Scottish caps. Willie Ormond was replaced as Scotland manager by Ally MacLeod, and the change, along with the suspension helped to make me the forgotten man of Scottish football. Little did I realise it then, but that sending-off in Prague was to send me into the wilderness for two years. I had to wait until September 1978 to put on the blue Scottish jersey again.

I suppose that night in Prague was one of the worst of my career, and a few weeks later I found myself in even deeper water with the English FA. It wasn't a sending-off but in many people's eyes, my crime was even worse. Villa were playing Manchester United in the first division at Villa Park and once again I lost control of my emotion for a split second, which was long enough to make an obscene "V" sign to the United fans. They had been on my back for most of the game, singing and chanting silly songs, but that was no excuse for my action. At the time I was so angry and tired of their constant barracking, that when we scored I waved both hands and four fingers in their direction. Unfortunately, a photographer had caught me making the gesture and the following Monday morning I was told off by the *Sun* newspaper for being so stupid. "Oh Andy. You're a super player – don't become a yob," was the headline. The papers reckoned my two finger sign had revealed a serious flaw in my character which could possibly stunt a most promising career. Coming so soon after the sending-off in Prague, they reckoned I was turning into something of a renegade. Lunatic behaviour, someone else called it and I was pilloried for denigrating my own considerable talent. I could not deny making the gesture, but the article made me angry for two reasons: first the whole incident was taken out of context and blown up beyond all proportion; and secondly it landed me in trouble with the FA. The paper reckoned I need not have made the "V" sign because Villa won 3-2 and by scoring two of these goals I had more than made my message of defiance towards the United fans. But when I lost my temper Villa had just equalised and the crowd had been slaughtering me. Admittedly it was a silly thing to do, and as soon as I did it I regretted it, of course, but it was hardly worth the headlines it received.

The match itself was a cracker, with five goals and plenty of action. I thought the paper was irresponsible in its own way by concentrating all of its report on just one split second and turning its back on all the excitement. Certainly the headlines captured the attention of the FA who, on reading the article and studying the photograph, summoned me to appear before the Disciplinary Committee on a charge of bringing the game into disrepute. I was given a personal hearing, when I admitted I had made the obscene gesture to the crowd, told them I deeply regretted it later and was sorry for what I'd done. After hearing my mitigating plea the FA sent me outside while they considered what sentence to pass. I could have faced a stiff ban, but the FA decided not to suspend me. Instead I was severely censured and fined £110. Not bad I suppose, it turned out at £27.50 a finger!

Seriously though, it taught me a lesson. I had to control my emotions and live up to the increasing responsibilities of being a top footballer. Until now I had been able to live my own life the way I wanted, but more and more I was becoming public property. People would stop and stare in the street, and it was almost impossible to go shopping or have a quiet night out without being invaded by football fans. The fame was all very nice, of course, and it made me realise that I owed it to myself to behave properly. When I was a kid, I worshipped the Rangers players, and realised how strong an influence I had on the young Villa supporters who would wait for hour upon hour for an autograph or a quick word from their favourite player. From those early flare-ups I like to think I have behaved myself better and never set anything but a good example. My main desires after all were to play well and entertainingly, and enjoy myself at the same time. Happily the sending-off and the "V" sign saga were the only two dark moments of that golden year. Villa were playing in front of packed houses everywhere they went and there were few sides who could stop us. Arsenal were demolished 5-1 at Villa Park, but the most rewarding result of all was yet to come.

In the middle of December, Liverpool were setting the pace at the top of the first division, closely followed by Ipswich, Manchester City, Newcastle and then Aston Villa. Six points separated us from Liverpool, and the biggest challenge of the season came on a Wednesday night game against the Anfield men. We had lost just one of our last nine games in the first division, and on top of that were through to the semi-finals of the League Cup. Also, we'd just come back from Elland Road where I'd scored two goals in a 3-1 victory over Leeds United. So the Villa confidence was soaring. Liverpool under Bob Paisley were driving forward as strong as ever, and had been beaten only once in their last eleven League games. The scene was set for a battle, and the Birmingham public responded as just under 43,000 of them greeted the teams as they ran out onto the pitch that night. Our last defeat had been to Liverpool at Anfield a few weeks earlier, and we were all determined, not only to avenge that but prove we were championship material by beating the trophy holders. It was a night I know the devoted Villa fans still treasure. We didn't just beat the champions, we annihilated them, winning 5-1. I got two, as did John Deehan, with my old partner Brian Little getting the other. It was a supreme performance by anyone's standards, and for poor old Liverpool it was their worst defeat in years. What's more astonishing is that all the goals came in the first half and it's a wonder we didn't finish up with ten that night such was our form. A victory over a side like Liverpool is always something to treasure, usually because of its rarity value, and there are not many goalscorers who'll go to the grave having helped fire five past the reds.

But that season Villa could do no wrong. In January we scaled even greater heights. In the FA Cup we swept aside both Leicester City and West Ham United to reach the fifth round, but the real achievement came a few weeks later in the League Cup when we reached Wembley. It took three matches and three hundred minutes of absorbing football in the semi-final against Queens Park Rangers before we finally made it. And on March 16th, 1977 Aston Villa were off to Wembley Stadium to play Everton in the League Cup Final. Everything was happening so fast, and for me the run up to the League Cup was an enjoyable time, but also a painful one. For several weeks I had been carrying an injury and was forced to miss League matches while I concentrated on getting fit for the semi-finals and then, of course, the final.

This was the start of Ron Saunders' play at any price policy, which earned me the tag of being injury prone, and could well have done some long term damage as well. Saunders was desperate for me to play in the League Cup matches, although I didn't consider myself to be one hundred per cent fit. He knew how badly I wanted to play and used my enthusiasm as a weapon against me. Often I would play, only to finish up in pain, but the Villa manager just wanted to see my name on the team sheet before the kick-off. He reckoned having me at number nine was always a physcological boost for Villa, even if I wasn't fully fit. At the time I went along with his methods because I was young, still relatively inexperienced, and of course desperately keen to do well. I didn't realise it at the time, but the foundations were being laid for my big bust-up with the Villa manager over injuries. Strange to think that in the middle of my golden year the blue fuse paper had been lit for the controversial end to my career at Villa Park under Ron Saunders.

Back in 1977 though, we were one happy family as we drove down Wembley Way to face Everton in the League Cup Final. We had already beaten them twice that season, and were considered as favourites to win. The occasion was a memorable one for me because it was my first match at Wembley. To a true Scot Hampden Park is the real home of soccer memories, but there's no escaping the unparalleled excitement that Wembley generates. Even though the League Cup didn't rate as highly as the more prestigious FA Cup, when a hundred thousand fans fill the stadium, it's still an occasion to remember. The best of the final was arriving in the coach as it slowly crawled towards the twin towers and thousands of Villa fans in their best claret and blue colours made for the match. Walking out for the pitch inspection with still an hour to go, you were deafened by the roar of the crowd. One of the banners at the Villa end proudly proclaimed. "Even Grecian 2000 Can't Stop Gray," and another said "Andy Gray Strikes More Than Leyland," which in those days was quite a claim! It was almost sad to leave the pitch for the dark dressing rooms which lie deep underneath the stadium. In there nerves and tension slowly took hold and what a relief it was to walk out of the tunnel at last to another blast of singing and cheering from the crowd. Sadly from there the day went downhill. The match finished in a goalless draw, and to be honest, it was an anti-climax. Neither side did justice to themselves, and I was so disappointed with myself at the end, that only twenty-one players made the lap of honour . . . I headed back to the dressing room alone. The Wembley officials wanted both teams to run around the stadium, and they tried to persuade me to go but I refused. In my mind I felt as though we had let the crowd down by dishing up a boring game, and had no right to run around on a victory type parade. So I went off on my own while the others did their lap of honour. Although the final was to be replayed on the Wednesday night, the feeling I had as I walked off that day was not too dissimilar to the one I'd had with Dundee United when we lost to Celtic in the final of the Scottish Cup at Hampden. Then, you remember, I threw my medal away in the dressing room, now I was walking off empty handed again. This time though, I didn't have to wait long for a pick-me-up . . . within twenty-four hours I was given two of football's most glittering prizes.

The day after the League Cup Final the PFA, The Professional Footballers Association, were holding their annual dinner and awards ceremony in London. Some of the Aston Villa lads had been planning to go to London that night for the dinner, but with a replay against Everton on Wednesday coming up, it had been decided to stop at home and watch the highlights on the television. After the League Cup Final I was still in trouble with an injury and was down for a few days of treatment before the replay. On Sunday morning I was at home in Birmingham reading through the reports of the final the day before when the phone rang. It was a call from London; Derek Dougan, chairman of the PFA and secretary Cliff Lloyd had some incredible news; I'd been voted Player of the Year and Young Player of the Year by my fellow professionals. Never before, or since, come to that, has a player won both awards. I was stunned by the news because, although I'd read somewhere I was on the shortlist to be nominated Young Player of the Year, I had forgotten all about it, what with the League Cup Final and everything else.

There was a snag though. I wasn't planning to go to the dinner in London, and what's more Ron Saunders had apparently refused permission for me to go because of my injury. This threw the PFA into a panic. They had the awards in London but not the winner and Derek Dougan, the Doog, wanted to know if there was any way I could make it on my own. Doog wondered if I could put pressure on Ron Saunders to let me attend the dinner that night. It was important for me to be there, as it was being televised on ITV. I told them my hands were tied and I had to stand by whatever the Villa manager had decided. About half an hour later they rang back. In the meantime, they'd approached Ron Saunders again for permission to let me go, and even tried to get the club chairman Sir William Dugdale involved. Doog came on and said "Look Andy we're in a real mess. We've got to have you down here, so if we sent a car for you, or even arranged a flight from Birmingham, is there any chance you could make it?" What they wanted me to do was go against the orders of Ron Saunders and travel to London to the awards ceremony behind his back. Now, at the time I didn't fully appreciate just how important the awards were, and was definitely not going to risk landing myself in trouble with the manager on the eve of a League Cup Final replay. If it happened again now, under the same circumstances, I'd jump in my car and head south, but then I was younger and much more cautious. "I'm sorry Derek, if the boss says I'm not to go then I can't risk it," was what I told the PFA chairman. I thought that was the end of it, but a few moments later the Doog rang back and this time he made me an offer which had my blood boiling "Andy we're in a very embarrassing position down here. With you up there, we haven't got anyone to pick up the awards, and it's not going to look good. We've been wondering is there any chance you could give up one of your awards and we'll give it to someone else." For a moment I was nearly caught off guard and said yes, but the more I thought about it the crosser I got. "Hold on Derek, if the players have voted for me, then it's only right that I should get the awards ... I'm not going to be part of any fix." And that was that I thought. What was the point of all the professionals from the ninety-two League clubs sitting down to vote for their Player of the Year if the PFA were going to give the award to someone who could make it to the dinner and

stand in front of the television camera? A little later the Doog
was back, and this time he wanted to know whether I'd have
any objection if the cameras came round to my house and
filmed me receiving one of the awards. They were prepared to
send the trophy up from London and get one of the Villa players
to make the presentation. That suited me fine so, later on, my
home was invaded by the television technicians. There were
vans, and even a jeep parked in the drive as directors, camera-
men and engineers tramped in and out. With enough lights to
outshine the Blackpool illuminations, all the neighbourhood
came down to see what was going on. Chris Nicholl, the Villa
skipper, made the presentation to me and it was relayed and
shown in London where all the rest of the players had gathered
for the big night. It wasn't until the following year when I had
the chance to go to the dinner I realised how much I'd missed
out by not being there at the presentation. Two things happened
because of the Sunday. First of all the PFA changed the rules, so
the same player could not win both awards, and I had to move
house!

Not many poeple knew where I lived before then, but so
much commotion was caused by the television people that word
soon got round, and from that day on there was a procession of
people knocking at my door. Most of them meant well, some
wanted an autograph or picture, but others would call early in
the morning, or even last thing at night. I enjoyed being popular
and didn't mind signing autographs, but it was essential to have
somewhere to unwind and switch off away from the game. So, I
decided to move house to get a little more privacy.

After that Sunday there was disappointment for me. First
Villa drew again in the League Cup Final replay with Everton
at Sheffield Wednesday's Hillsborough ground, and then I was
carried off in a League match at Derby County with ligament
trouble. My leg was put in plaster, and it meant missing the
second Cup Final replay at Old Trafford, which happily Villa
won 3-2 after extra time. I was overjoyed for the lads, but no
matter how good the team spirit, you never get the same sense of
achievement if you haven't played in the game yourself.

I was back in the team for the end of the season and rounded off a great year with a hat-trick in the last match against West Bromwich Albion. Those three goals made me joint top scorer in the first division along with Arsenal's Malcolm Macdonald. On top of that Villa had won the League Cup and a place in Europe after finishing fourth in the first division – their best performance and finish for forty-four years. Added to which Andy Gray had won the Player and Young Player of the Year Awards. Yes that really was a Golden Year – one I would dearly love to live again.

7 DON'T CRY FOR ME ARGENTINA

The highs and lows of football have always been difficult to contend with, and for some players they prove too much. It's easy to be swept away in your own success, and be drowned despairingly as fortunes suddenly change. I've suffered more ups and downs than most in my career. The initial success at Villa was followed by two fallow years of injuries and argument. Then came Wolves, and at first success with a League Cup win at Wembley, but soon after a drop to division two. The next high was joining Everton and playing a part in their glorious comeback to the top, but no sooner had the cheers died down then I was on the move again . . . back to Aston Villa. I think I've managed to take everything in my stride and obeyed the code set by Rudyard Kipling which has been held up to many sporting champions: "If you can meet with Triumph and Disaster and treat those two imposters just the same."

Coming from relatively lowly beginnings in Drumchapel as I did, the chance to play football is a wonderful gift and whenever the bad times come along I ride through them by thinking how lucky I've been. Although I was glad to get out of Drumchapel to see more of life, I still go back there whenever I can to meet the many friends who've stayed by my side from the early schooldays. Having friends back home away from football has helped keep my feet on the ground as well as staying in touch with everyday life.

In my early days at Villa, whenever I felt under pressure or depressed by injury, I would resort to my early morning cure. I'd get up and leave home at the unearthly hour of six o'clock and drive down to the main bus depot in Birmingham, and there I would sit for at least an hour watching the local people go to work. The shift workers bound for the car assembly plants would be wiping the sleep from their eyes, the women cleaners would be dragging their shopping bags along the pavement, while the roadsweepers would stir slowly into another day. I sat and watched them, not to gloat, but to show myself how fortunate I was. While they toiled away day in, day out, and tramped to their work benches in all weather, I was by comparison living a life of luxury. Up at nine, training at ten, and home by one. I had my moans and groans, of course, don't we all, but my troubles or problems paled into insignificance as I sat watching the Birmingham people go to work.

Mind you, there were still occasions when I felt sorry for myself, and none worse than the end of the 1977-78 season when I was left out of the World Cup squad. To play for my country in the World Cup was, and sadly still is, a burning ambition. Having been suspended after that punch-up in Prague, I'd missed the rest of Scotland's build-up to Argentina and was trying desperately hard to prove my fitness and form to the national manager Ally MacLeod who'd taken over in the summer of 1977. I kicked off the season with another encouraging run of form which brought nine goals in nine games, including two against the champions Liverpool at Anfield. Villa became the first team to win there for nearly two years and my goals even earned a rousing reception from the famous Kop. At that time I was having trouble with a back injury. I couldn't touch my toes and slept on a wooden board every night, but somehow managed to summon up enough steam to challenge the first division defences. The season, in general, was a disappointing one as Villa never fulfilled the promise we'd shown in the year before. By and large the team was the same with Jimmy Rimmer having arrived from Arsenal to take over in goal, and skipper Chris Nicholl being replaced by Ken McNaught of Everton. One blow came when Alex Cropley broke his leg badly in a derby game with West Bromwich Albion. In the competitions we made it to the fourth round in the League Cup, but fell at the first hurdle in the FA Cup and the only real success came with a run to the quarter finals of the UEFA Cup where Barcelona finally knocked us out. I missed the Barcelona game through injury, but was back in the team again for the final run into the first division League programme.

Ally MacLeod was due to name his World Cup pool of forty players in March and although I hadn't played for the national side in nearly eighteen months, I was still regarded as a must by most of the Scottish supporters. Sure enough, I was in the World Cup pool which meant I then had a couple of months to prove to Ally MacLeod I was worth a place in his final squad of twenty-two. It was reassuring to read the papers, who all looked in their crystal balls to predict the squad that would carry the nation's hopes to Argentina. More than anything I was desperate to make amends for being sent off in Prague at the start of the qualifying rounds when I feared I might have ruined Scotland's hopes of reaching the finals. Fortunately, they'd pulled through as clear winners of their group, with a famous win over Wales at Liverpool's Anfield ground, finally clinching a trip to South America.

My main rivals for a place in the final squad were Joe Harper of Aberdeen and Rangers' Derek Johnstone. Kenny Dalglish and Joe Jordan were automatic choices and at one stage, I must confess I thought I was, looking at my scoring record compared to others. That wise Scottish soccer scribe Hugh McIlvanney went in print to advise Ally MacLeod that the names of Gray, Dalglish and full-back Danny McGrain should be the first on the team sheet for Argentina. "Andy Gray is a genuine phenomenon, the best centre forward British football has seen in years, its most thrilling front player since Denis Law went into decline. He is strong, brave, agile, perceptive, quick and relentlessly hard on himself and he finishes with killing simplicity in the air or on the ground. He is a defender's nightmare and a manager's dream and if Scotland fail to use him properly in the World Cup it will be a crime," he wrote.

What better reference could a man ask for I thought, and towards the end of the 1978 season I had my sights set on one thing . . . a World Cup place and a ticket to Argentina. All went well and Ally MacLeod let it be known he was going to watch me in Villa's match against West Bromwich Albion at their

Hawthorns ground. We were convincing 3-0 winners, and although I failed to score I still felt I'd done enough to show the Scotland manager I was worth a place in his squad. The most important thing was to prove my fitness. I'd been out with torn ligaments but played in the last eleven games of the season by which time I felt I was ready. On the day the squad was due to be announced I took myself away from home deliberately, not being able to bear the long wait by the phone. When squads are announced the press usually get to know before the players do and I was hoping for a call from the local paper seeking my reaction to being picked. The wait though would have killed me, so off I went to a wine bar, which a pal of mine ran in Birmingham City centre. Come lunchtime he volunteered to go and call a local reporter to find out news of the squad. Off he went, and I prayed for his return and some glad tidings. He didn't have to say a word when he came back, I knew by the look on his face the news was bad. "They've not picked you in the squad Andy. They've gone and bloody well left you out," were the words that burnt into my mind. I was stunned into silence. That was perhaps the biggest blow I've ever suffered in football. How on earth, I thought, could I have been left out? I know I'd been sent off and then banned, but that was way in the past and surely I'd played well enough and scored enough goals since then to prove my worth. I just couldn't believe it and my shock quickly turned into anger. If Ally MacLeod, the Scotland team manager, had happened to walk into that wine bar then, I swear I would have punched him from there right back to Glasgow. What annoyed me even more was that he'd seen fit to include Manchester United centre half Gordon McQueen in the squad even though he had ligament trouble. As it turned out Gordon never played. That summer when Scotland took off for Argentina I felt bitter and bewildered; I had to force myself to watch the games on television and, although deeply disappointed with the team's performances, I still felt I could have helped Scotland achieve much more than they did in Argentina. As it turned out the World Cup was such a disaster that shortly afterwards Ally MacLeod resigned to take over as manager of Ayr. I can't say I was sorry. He had caused me the biggest heartache of my international career, but he wasn't the only manager to cause me problems that year.

Back at Villa Park my relationship with Ron Saunders had turned sour and my break from the club had started. Ironic really, because at the start of the season I was one of the four players who formed a deputation to persuade the Villa manager to stay with the club. After our League Cup win and a promising run in the first division, Ron Saunders had been offered a lucrative deal to go to one of the oil capitals in the Middle East where such men as Don Revie, the former England manager, were earning vast amounts of money. One morning at training, Saunders called the first team squad together and told us about the offer. He wanted the players to discuss it and let him know what they thought. Looking back, he was probably using us as a weapon against the Villa board, but at the time the players were right behind him, and after a team meeting four of us went along to his office at the training ground to ask him to stay. We never heard any more about the Arabian offer, and gradually Ron Saunders gathered power. The team's success had strengthened his position as manager and Ron Saunders slowly took control of the club. He wanted total control, and it was that policy which was finally his undoing at Villa Park.

Not satisfied with just being manager, Saunders wanted a say in anything and everything that went on at the club, whether it involved the players or not, and heaven help anyone who tried to go against him. He loved yes men, and tried to rule Aston Villa with a rod of iron, although I often suspected his bark was far more fiercesome than his bite. Many of the club's characters were discarded because he appeared to hate too much attention lavished on one player. He was a strong believer in his team, and that's fair enough, but when success comes to a club it's only natural that some players attract more attention or grab bigger headlines than others. He resented this and quite often, in my case, would try to stop me talking to local reporters or giving interviews on radio and television. I suppose his argument would be that he was trying to guard players from getting too big for their boots and at the same time preserve a state of equilibrium in the dressing room. That's all well and good, but most of the men at Villa Park were capable of looking after themselves and no one man had the right to dictate the way you should lead your life. Any hint of flamboyance would be quickly stamped out and I think in the long run the club suffered. I can always remember the treatment that was dished out by Saunders to goalkeeper Jimmy Cumbes who'd been one of the promotion winning team and also a member of the side which won the League Cup in 1975. Jimmy, who was a skilled cricketer as well and served both Worcestershire and Warwickshire after his football days, was a lively, jovial and very friendly man. He was not a Ron Saunders man though, because he would challenge something if he thought it wrong. So Jimmy and another great character Pat McMahon were cast aside by Saunders who made them train alone. It was as if Saunders feared the rest of the players being influenced by them and we used to call the lonely training sessions for the outcasts "Jim Cumbes Leper Colony".

If you study the comings and goings at Villa Park in the Saunders' years, you'll find that more often than not the players that departed were lively, colourful, independent sort of people who had something more about them and were not just running machines. That was the way Aston Villa was going. It was very much Ron Saunders' way. You have to applaud the man for eventually taking the League Championship, a great achievement, but I didn't agree with his methods and would never play for him again. He believed in pushing the players hard in training, too hard at times, and one of the best quotes on Ron Saunders' policy came from no less a figure than Bill Shankly, that great manager of Liverpool. I talked a lot with him when I was moving to Wolves and Shankly was clearly no admirer of Ron Saunders' methods. "He'll kill you the way he's driving you. I can't understand the way he runs people. In all my life I've yet to see a football pitch with a one in four gradient." A typical Shankly remark. Apart from the hill running and endless physical work in training, Ron Saunders also put pressure on me to play when I wasn't really fit, and this was eventually the reason I left Aston Villa.

I'll never forget the time I spent virtually the whole week flat on my back in hospital and ended up playing in a derby match against Birmingham City the day after I'd checked myself out of the clinic. The club doctor had sent me to hospital on the Sunday for treatment on a twinge I'd had in my back. It was decided to put me in traction and for days I was forced to lay still on my back in bed. Now I've never been one to stay in the same place for too long and by Thursday I was absolutely fed up. I hadn't had a good night's sleep in four days so I decided I was going home. I managed to pull myself out of bed and as I was undoing all the weights which had been keeping me flat out the nurses came running into the room. "What do you think you're doing?" they said. "I've had enough. I can't stand it any more, I've got to go." "But you can't," they skrieked. "You can't just walk out while you're under treatment Mr Gray." "Do you want to bet?" I said "Just watch me. I'm going home for a good sleep and if the doctor wants me he knows where to find me." And off I marched home. Like a fool I was back at Villa the next day and allowed Ron Saunders to talk me into being substitute.

It was the derby game against Birmingham City, a match we had to win more for the prestige than the points. I can hear Ron Saunders now: "Look Andy, it'll give the fans a bit of a boost if they see you on the team sheet, and it might just worry the Blues a bit as well." So I went along with his wishes after he'd promised me I'd only be called upon in an emergency. Lo and behold with five minutes gone Brian Little limped off and Villa were down to ten men. It meant, of course, that I had to go on. So, on a day I should by rights still have been on my back in hospital I found myself pitched into one of the full-blooded battles of Birmingham.

I've lost count of the number of times I played for Villa carrying an injury of one sort of another. In hindsight I was stupid. Playing with injuries invariably made them worse and eventually led to me missing more and more games. If I had been allowed to recover naturally and fully from injury, I'm convinced I would not have missed as many games as I did at Villa Park under Ron Saunders. Frequently I played with pain-killing injections. The doctor would pump them into me half an hour before kick-off, and out I would go unable sometimes to even feel my legs. My ankles were at times so heavily strapped that it was like playing in a heavy pair of diver's boots. There was never any mention of it in public, of course. A headline like "Andy Gray Passes a Last Minute Fitness Test" usually meant I'd had a painkiller just before kick-off and a heavy bandage wrapped tightly around the injury. The injections invariably wore off before the end of the match and then the pain, worse than ever, would grip like an ever tightening vice. As long as Villa were winning though and I was starting as number nine, Ron Saunders was happy. Eventually I realised just how much damage the injections and playing on injuries could be causing me.

So since those Villa days I've refused to have painkillers. They are the scourge of the modern game. It's often said in dressing rooms that horses have better treatment than humans, and it's true as far as some football clubs go. It's fair enough risking a slight injury or a doubtful ankle say for a big match, but too many clubs try it on too often and expect players to sacrifice their future health. In a way you are cheating, not only yourself, but your teammates and supporters, who rightly expect a player to give everything he's got in a game. Sometimes because of injury a player can't do it but that's never explained to the folk on the terraces. Happily, most clubs, especially first and second division sides, have tightened up on their medical care in recent seasons. But I could still name you a team of class players whose careers finished early because they were abused so badly. A specialist told me not so long ago that because of all the knocks and injuries I'd suffered through the years there was no way I'd still be playing first-class football when I'm thirty-four. Some may say that the injuries have come as a direct result of the way I go in where angels fear to tread. I've never kidded myself about the high risk element of my job, but what I am saying now is that had I been allowed a little more time to recover in the past the old legs might just be in a bit better shape now. It's a topic I feel strongly about and that's why indirectly it led to my argument with Saunders. I say argument, but strangely enough we never actually crossed swords. It was something Ron Saunders said behind my back that caused the rift between us.

It happened in March 1978 when Villa faced Barcelona in the quarter finals of the UEFA Cup. We were going well in Europe that season and had reached the last eight after three tough matches: first we beat the Turkish side Fenerbahce, then Gornik Zabrze of Poland and finally in the third round had squeezed through against the Spanish Athletico Bilbao. Before the Barcelona game I'd picked up an injury and missed the first leg at Villa Park which finished in a 2-2 draw. The return leg was two weeks later, and the race was on to get fit for the trip to Spain. All the players were convinced they still had a chance of snatching a result in the awe-inspiring Nou Camp Stadium. It was a match I was desperate to play in. Not every day did you get the chance to compete against such world legends as Johan Cruff and Johan Neeskens, who were the star attractions of the Barcelona team. Every day I had treatment on my thigh strain up at Villa's training ground, where Ron Saunders would anxiously check how I was recovering.

On the Sunday before Villa were due to fly out for Spain I was forced to pull out. There was no way I could fool myself. The strain was still painful and too bad to play on. The Villa manager pressed me to give it a go and I would have dearly loved to have said yes and taken my place in the team, but deep down I knew I couldn't make it. If I had gone I would have been cheating the rest of the Villa team because the risk was too great. I would have been useless passenger; if we were to win we needed eleven good men and true.

However, it was Saunders' reaction that really hurt and caused all the trouble. He let it be known he was disgusted with the way I'd let him down by not playing against Barcelona. He called me a cheat behind my back and reckoned I'd chickened out of the return leg which Villa lost. I was enraged at this. In all my life I have never cheated anyone and in football I have never given less than my all. After everything I had done for Villa I felt this was a wicked slur on my character, and from that day to this have never fully forgiven Ron Saunders for what he said. I never confronted him, because at the time I didn't think it would have served much purpose. He had repaid my loyalty to him and the club by insulting me, and from then on our relationship went down hill. It was this cheating allegation that eventually led to my departure from Villa Park. I knew I could never be happy again playing for a manager who'd branded me a cheat and it took a long time after I left Villa Park even to talk to Ron Saunders. We passed each other at games without saying a word until eventually, after one match against his new team Birmingham City, I decided it was time to break the silence. I asked him about his family and we passed the time of day, but that was all. Ron Saunders was good to me when I first arrived at Villa Park, and to give him due credit he has a fine record as a manager. His style and methods are not mine, and it's safe to say we'll never team up again.

The following season, 1978-79, turned out to be my last at Villa Park and it was probably the worst as well. I played in just eighteen matches all season with injury making me miss much of the action. First I suffered a thigh strain at the start of the season, but the worst came in a League cup tie against Luton Town at Villa Park. Early on in the first half I got caught in a strong tackle and down I went in agony. It was the right knee again. I'd had one operation on it in my first season at Dundee United and knew from the minute I crashed to the ground against Luton that the injury was much more than just an ordinary knock. After the doctor, physio and specialist had all examined it thoroughly it was decided I needed another cartilage operation, and that kept me out of action from November to the begining of March. Of all matches to make a comeback in I chose the derby game with Birmingham City, but at least we won, although the knee was still giving me trouble. I tried to forget about the pain and persuade myself it ws just stiffness, but deep down I could feel it still wasn't right. I played on though and scored a couple of goals, one at home to Bolton and the other against Spurs at White Hart Lane, which as it turned out was my last for Aston Villa. My final game in the claret and blue was against Nottingham Forest at the City Ground. It wasn't a happy ending as we lost 4-0 and my right knee was still causing concern for both myself and the medical men. I was disappointed and a little worried when the specialist decided the knee needed yet another operation, the third in five years.

At first there was a scare my knee could be seriously weakened, and although the specialist was confident another operation would clear the problem it was still a nervous time. Whenever you get a cartilage of ligament problem, you know in the back of your mind that such an injury is capable of claiming a career. And when I went into hospital I know there were several doubting Thomases around football saying I was finished, or injury prone.

When you look back on my record at Villa I played more matches than many think I did. In four seasons I made 112 League appearances for the Villa and knocked in fifty-five goals, and in twenty-nine cup matches scored fifteen times. Sixty-nine goals in 141 matches averages out at nearly a goal in every other game which to my way of thinking is a very respectable record. Although I'd played my last match for Villa in April 1979 there was still plenty of action to come. I was back in training at the start of the next season all right, when the Andy Gray transfer saga brought about some of the most bizarre scenes I've ever been involved in. But before all that, it was time to enjoy myself and live life a little more daringly.

8 A WHOLE NEW BALL GAME

They always say all work and no play makes Jack a dull boy. No danger of them saying that about Andy though, because along the way I've certainly enjoyed some richly entertaining years. I've always like to think of myself as a dedicated sportsman and have never neglected the game, but at the same time I've managed to take time out to enjoy myself. For one reason or another I earned quite a celebrity tag when at Villa, and a lot of that was down to my first big business venture, as a night club owner. Derek Dougan, former PFA chairman and later my boss at Wolves, once wrote a book about how not to run a football club. I could easily match that with "How not to run a night club". We had a lot of fun, but eventually I ended up losing around £40,000 which taught me a valuable lesson in life. At the time I was twenty-two and earning an awful lot of money, something like £400 a week. Financial advisers reckoned I should invest some of it for later years and there was no shortage of offers. Each football club has something in common – hangers-on. Success of course brings them by the barrow load, but as in showbusiness or any other branch of entertainment people love to be seen with the stars. And Villa attracted more than it's fair share of followers.

Villa, as I've pointed out before, has always been Birmingham's most fashionable club. On match day the car park would be crammed with Rolls Royces and Mercedes and in the guest lounges there was always a fragrance of expensive perfume. It was quite something to be seen on the day of the game at Villa mixing with the cream of the second city's sporting society. There were, of course, some very pleasant and

101

genuine people, but hangers-on were there as well and a young footballer can easily be led astray. I wouldn't say I was, because I made sure my business never affected my football, but at twenty-two I was still naive and easy meat for the big game hunters who came offering a golden business opportunity. I'd already turned down several money making ventures which I didn't fancy when some pals of mine at the time put forward the idea of opening a night club. They, along with two others, would provide the business acumen and attend to the day-to-day running, while my name would be used to sell the idea to the public. It was an exciting idea and one I thought which would catch on. Birmingham's nightlife was way behind that of London's, of course, and even places like Manchester and Leeds had more clubs and restaurants. Sixty thousand pounds was needed to get the business going and we were lucky to find some premises just off the city centre in Livery Street.

The premises were originally part of the old Snow Hill station and in estate agents terms ripe for development and modernisation. Our plan was to provide a sophisticated night club where the food, surroundings and company were a cut above the average. Builders and decorators set to work to convert the old station into a luxurious nightspot: we were going to have a tasteful but stylish decor, softly lit lounges, with quiet music playing in the background, a five star restaurant, a disco area and also a room to put on cabaret shows from time to time. We decided it would be called "The Holy City Zoo" after the world famous club in San Francisco which had always been the haunt of the rich and famous in California.

The first blow or setback came before we opened with two of my four partners pulling out. So much work had been put into the project, the three of us who were left decided we should go ahead with our plans and open the first human zoo in Birmingham. My elder brother Duncan agreed to join me and manage the club with another old Glasgow boy, the legendary Rab Jackson, helping out behind the bar as well. I say legendary because the story of how Rab came to Birmingham has been told a thousand times over and his fame has spread so much that when he was introduced to Liverpool's goal machine Ian

Rush not so long ago, even the Anfield ace asked him wide-eyed in admiration if it was THE Rab Jackson he was shaking hands with! Rab and I had been through a few scrapes as kids back home in Glasgow and I always kept in touch with all my mates from those Drumchapel days. Poor old Rab had been having a bit of an unhappy time at home so, in the hope of cheering him up, I asked him down to stay for the weekend ... and nine years later would you believe, he's still here. Rab liked it so much he's never bothered to go back home and is still enjoying the longest weekend break of his life. With him and Duncan working at the club I was confident all would go well. Despite my differences with Ron Saunders he had no objection to me branching out as long as it didn't interfere with my work or performances with Villa. Surprise, surprise he even let me off early from a night game to go to the grand opening in March 1979. We were playing Bolton at Villa Park on that Wednesday night and at half-time we were 3-0 up and cruising to victory. I'd got one of the goals, ironically my last at Villa Park as it turned out, but was suffering with my right knee. In the dressing room at half-time they had a look at it and Ron Saunders told me not to bother going out after the break. He was confident of a win and would use the substitute for the second half. So he told me to get changed and go and open my club; a very generous gesture and a surprising one on his part, but at the time deeply appreciated. And that night the champagne flowed as the Holy City Zoo opened its doors for business. The opening had been well advertised and covered by the local papers and with Villa winning that night as well the celebrations went on into the early hours.

For the first few months the Zoo went well. The guests read like a who's who of the entertainment world: Billy Connolly, another Drumchapel kid of course, always dropped in when he was in town; the Three Degrees were regulars as well; we had the Drifters, Jim Davidson, Russ Abbott, Bernie Winters and many many more. The Zoo was the place to be seen, and we had a few memorable nights and mornings as the fun spread into the early hours. We didn't finish one party until dawn one weekend but I had to be careful and not be dragged into wicked ways. I was well aware that if my game should suffer, only slightly, people would be quick to point an accusing finger at me. So I went to the club only two nights a week. Saturday, of course, after the game was always a time to either celebrate or drown your sorrows and if there were no midweek matches I'd try to have a Tuesday or Wednesday down there. I rarely got involved in the actual running of the club and was concious once again it would be wrong to see a footballer behind the bar pulling pints and dispensing tots of whisky.

Mind you, we weren't short for staff and we even had a few celebrities helping out at times. Birmingham comedian Dave Ismay, an old friend and diehard Villa supporter, would often lend a hand but had a most unusual way of serving. Dave could never remember the prices of the different drinks and so charged everyone a pound no matter what they had. A bottle of champagne, a pint of bitter, a double scotch or even an orange juice or lemonade were all a pound. Amazingly we just about broke even when he was serving and with Dave playing mine host the Zoo could proudly boast it served the cheapest bubbly, but the most expensive orange juice in all of Birmingham.

And never did the champagne flow more freely than the night of my twenty-fourth birthday. We decided to hold the party to end all parties, and that night it seemed as though the whole of Birmingham was celebrating. In the entrance hall we fixed up a solid silver fountain which gushed with champagne all night. The idea was for the guests to come in and help themselves to a glass but someone, probably me, forgot to switch the fountain off after everyone had been welcomed and the bubbly flowed into the early hours of the morning.

When it came to drinking one of the regulars was the champion of all time. Everyone knew him as Slim. At 5' 10" and 20 stone he always stood out in a crowd and, although he worked at another Birmingham night club, Slim would often find his way to the Zoo. The legend was that Slim could drink any man under the table and tales were told of how he could drink up to thirty pints of lager in one session. One night he was in early and we got talking about his record and foolishly I challenged him to see if he could beat it there and then. The bet was that if Slim beat the record I'd pay for the beer but if he failed, he would have to cough up. I must add that I was just a bystander as Slim started out to drink pint after pint after pint. He started to slow down at thirty around midnight but then found his second wind and finished off by downing thirty-six pints of lager. Amazingly he got off his stool by the bar and calmly took a taxi home. To look at him or even chat to him you wouldn't have guessed that Slim had drunk more than a couple of pints and I reckon that's one feat the *Guinness Book of Records* missed out on. What a record breaker our Slim was! He was quite a character and at our expense became the talk of the town one time. People kept asking me in the club if Slim had come into money or won the pools as he'd been seen driving around the city in a spanking new Rolls Royce. We discovered that Slim had been craftily borrowing one of our customers cars. At night he would come down to the club to lend a helping hand and quite often one of our regulars would cruise up to the front door in his roller, throw the keys to Slim and ask him to park it. Unbeknown to us all Slim would jump in and cruise around the city in the car making sure he was seen by some of his pals. Thankfully he drove on the nights when he hadn't downed thirty-six pints and nobody ever guessed what he was up to. To this very day the owner is none the wiser, although his mileage to the gallon must have improved somewhat without Slim parking his car for him.

The Zoo was often so full on a weekend that people would queue down the street to get in. When two people left, two more were allowed in through the doors and on nights when it was quiet we devised another method to attract customers. We'd go off to some of the other local clubs armed with a pocketful of free passes and once we were inside hand them around. Within the hour the other clubs would slowly empty as the queue outside the Zoo built up. Sharp practice if you like, but there was always something to attract them to the club. One lady who pulled a full house was Fiona Richmond, the sex queen, who was performing at one of the local theatres. Along with some friends we'd been invited to her first night, and the opening line has to be one of the classics of all time. A naked lady walked onto the stage, and with the spotlight glaring down on her said, "Could I have your attention please!" Later on Fiona had all the attention she could handle. The men flocked around her like bees to a honey pot, and that night she left me with a signed picture: "To Andy, love and lust, Fiona."

I enjoyed the Zoo and it's good times immensely. It was a place I could go to relax and enjoy myself away from the glare of being a football star. Lots of other players from local clubs were welcomed as well for much the same reason, they knew they could have an undisturbed night out. Sadly the champagne went flat after a time and in a way I only had myself to blame. My brother Duncan kept telling me he wasn't happy about one or two things that were going on at the club involving the two other partners and kept asking me to take a closer look at things. Like a fool I ignored him. At the time I was busy with my football and had other problems on my plate to give the Zoo much thought. I suppose much of the initial delight of having a club had rubbed off and poor old Duncan's complaints fell on deaf ears. Finally after about eighteen months Duncan told me he has was packing in and going back home. "It's all wrong Andy. Things aren't being run as they should. I can't stop any longer," were Duncan's parting words. My mate Rab left as well and only when those two had gone did I finally come to my senses and get an accountant to take a close look at the business. The books were a right mess and Duncs was right, my two partners, so-called friends, had taken me for a ride. The club was deep in debt and losing more money by the minute. We tried to rescue it but in the end the Holy City Zoo shut up shop. It had been open for just over two years and with the other two partners gone as well by then I was left with a bill for £40,000. I paid up and put it down to experience, hoping it was the most expensive lesson I'll ever have to learn in life. As I said I was naive and had been a victim of the hangers-on. I trusted my business partners too much and should have paid more attention to the people that really mattered, Duncan and Rab.

It certainly put me off business for a time as well, although I could hardly afford another speculative venture with my club debts taking up all of my savings. If you've got to get caught like that I suppose it's best when you're young. It taught me a lesson all right and now the wounds have healed and all my debts paid off in full I can think about business more logically. If another chance came along I might even have another go, but next time I would be much more careful. I'd keep a close watch on the books, say from week to week, and be much more demanding on anyone who worked with me or for me. I should have known that business success is like football. You get out what you put in and at the Holy City Zoo too many people had too easy a time at my expense. The scars of failure are made less painful now when I look back and remember the parties and crazy nights we had down at the Zoo. I could have done without the final bill but wouldn't have missed the fun for anything. The club opened up a new world to me as the Drumchapel kid was invited down to London's West End and wined and dined in the millionaire's playground. Billy Connolly gave me tickets for his show in Drury Lane and later we hit the town by going to Tramps, the most exclusive and expensive club in the capital. Our old friends the Three Degrees were there as well and I suppose being seen at such places was why people jumped to the conclusion I was a bit wild and reckless. I loved to have a good time and unwind from the pressures of football but would challenge anyone who could find me guilty of neglect.

There was a time, just a few weeks after I'd been transferred to Wolves, when the press went made with a story about me walking barefoot through the streets of Birmingham. It was a hot September day and quite often in the summer when it gets really warm I discard my shoes and walk around with bare feet. One lunchtime I was having a coffee in Birmingham and spotted a traffic warden looking my car up and down. It was parked on a yellow line so I rushed out to move it before I got handed a ticket. Just my luck that a photographer from the local paper was passing by and spotted me walking across the road with no shoes on. Before I knew it the camera was clicking and suddenly the whole story snowballed. It was in the evening paper and some of the nationals the next day. What was Britain's most expensive footballer doing walking around with bare feet? Some suggested it was irresponsible. To me it was just a natural thing, although as one of my pals pointed out it might have been wiser to sit tight and get a parking ticket rather than run the gauntlet with the press. It was best summed up by John Barnwell, my manager at Wolves, who when asked for reaction about his new £1.5 million centre forward walking barefoot, laughed and said, "If Andy wants to walk around barefoot he can do so as far as I am concerned."

Barny knew me and what's more trusted me. I wasn't bothered about the publicity because through the years I've enjoyed a good working relationship with the press. I've been misquoted a few times but that's life, although once it led to a very embarassing moment. Hundreds of proposals of marriage from Turkish girls poured through my letter box after a joke backfired. It was just before Villa's game against Fenerbache in the UEFA cup. The Turks had brought over a large delegation of press with them and after a training session one morning they tracked me down for a press conference. As Villa's top goalscorer they reckoned me to be the danger man and thought I warranted some special attention. So, with the help of an interpreter, they asked me all about my life and what I thought our chances were in the cup game. They scribbled away in their notebooks as I rambled on and then one chap moved onto my personal life. Where do you come from? When did you start playing football? Just two of the questions he asked, and was I married? "Me married," I replied. "I'm single and have no plans to marry yet unless you've got any spare girls across there in Turkey," I joked. I suppose I should have known better because in translation from English to Turkish my flippant remark must have lost it's lightheartedness, although it wasn't until the postman came calling I realised how much damage I had done. One or two newspapers back in Turkey had taken my remark to mean I was thinking of getting married and was seriously interested in a Turkish girl. About a week or so later sacks of mail started arriving at Villa Park, all with a Turkish postmark. In all I must have received something like 600 letters and most contained proposals of marriage from young girls. Some had sent photographs of themselves because they had been convinced from reading their newspapers that I wanted to take a wife. One or two went into long detail of how they would look after me and pander to my every wish. I certainly had a laugh reading the letters, most of which were written in pidgeon English and to be honest I was flattered that so many girls should be interested in me. They all wanted to see me or even meet me when Villa travelled to Turkey for the second leg and suddenly I realised how much deep water I'd landed myself in. I didn't fancy being beseiged by hundreds of Turkish ladies although some looked quite delightful. By coincidence I was injured and unable to make the flight to Turkey the following week and frankly I can't say I was too disappointed!

I never cease to be amazed how fans can track you down. One summer my wife, Jan, and I were enjoying a holiday over in Canada with my brother James and his family. We went on an outing into the Rockies one day and stopped to enjoy a rest and a drink at a little restaurant some 8,000 feet up. The mist came down and we were trapped for a couple of hours, and as we chatted to while away the time I noticed a chap staring at us from across the restaurant. I took no notice until he got up and walked towards us. For a moment I thought he was a pal of my brother's, but as soon as he opened his mouth it was obvious he was from Birmingham. In a thick Brummie accent he pointed towards me and declared. "It's Andy Gray isn't it? Fancy seeing you here. Can I have your autograph?" Jan and I burst out laughing as James and his wife looked at each other in disbelief. There I was on the other side of the world, 8,000 feet up in the Rockies, and a Brummie wants my autograph.

A couple of years later the same sort of thing happened again, this time in Bangkok of all places. I'd gone on tour there with Everton after winning the FA Cup and one day full-back John Bailey and I decided to drift off on our own and head up river. We hired a little boat, packed a few bottles of lager and took along some tapes as well. The locals had told us a trip up the river to see the country and the little villages was a must, so off we floated in the sun for an idyllic afternoon out. As we made our way up river we passed the little shanty towns of straw and mud huts that make up Bangkok. We were in the middle of absolutely nowhere and enjoying every minute. The only problem was we ran out of lemonade and decided to pull into a village in the distance where we spotted what I suppose was the nearest Bangkok had to a corner shop. Just on the bank some lads dressed in tatty clothes were kicking a football about and as we went to the counter they ran to serve us. They had lemonade and as I was handing over our money one of them chirped out in broken English and in a thick Thai accent, "You Andy Gray . . . You Andy Gray Football." I was absolutely flabbergasted that little kids miles up the river in Bangkok should know me. John Bailey laughed and burst in by saying, "Yes you're right son He's Andy Gray all right and I'm the Gnasher – Number Three." The kids went wild with excitement and suddenly we found ourselves surrounded by hundreds of them shouting and waving. They must have been coming out of the woodwork, and John "The Gnasher" Bailey and I spent nearly an hour signing autographs. We should have really guessed that the western world was well known even in this remote little village. All the mud huts, which had the river as their front garden, proudly displayed a television aerial. They might have lacked some of the luxuries which we take for granted, but every home had a telly and all the villagers loved watching English football on the box. They had all watched the FA Cup Final and ever since that day I've always had fan mail from the Far East. It just goes to show that football knows no barriers and a soccer star never walks alone whether he's 8,000 feet up in the Rockies or miles down the river in the middle of the jungle.

One of the great things about being a footballer is that it can lead you into a life of opportunities and adventures which other people just dream about. One of the most exciting times I had came when I was recovering from my third knee operation in the summer of 1979. I was told by Villa to have a holiday and although they wanted me to take things fairly easy I had to get my knee right again and that meant some careful training. Just before the summer I'd met a Birmingham lad called Tony Iomi, a member of the famous Black Sabbath rock band. We got talking in a club one night and although Tony was not really a football fan he mentioned that another member of the group Geezer Butler was mad about Aston Villa. On the strength of that I was invited to join Black Sabbath in America. They were recording and touring over there and had rented a house in Bel

Air, one of the star-studded residential areas of California. As soon as my operation was over and I could move freely on my feet I was jetting off to the States for a couple of unforgettable weeks. Some of the group met me at the airport in Los Angeles and instead of jumping into a taxi they brought their own transport and what a set of wheels it was! I've never seen a bigger can in all my life; a long sleek and shiny cadillac drew up outside the airport terminal and I almost expected to see the President of America himself step out it was so impressive. Inside it was sheer luxury – I reckon it was just about as big as our old flat back in Drumchapel. It rolled silently through the streets of Los Angeles and I felt like a king as we made for the distant hills of Bel Air. Every house we passed was like a palace set in its own grounds and as we purred along the homes of the Hollywood stars slipped by until we reached the big black metal gates of the Sabbath's sumptuous residence. Without warning the gates slid open electronically as the chauffeur aimed the limousine at the great gateway, and the grounds were so big it felt like another five minutes before we pulled in front of the house. I say house, but even if you called it a mansion you would be underselling it. It was such a vast building that at first I had to ask which part Sabbath were renting. The lot, I was told. For two weeks they took me around the Californian scene and to the pop parties and receptions that were all part of their life. I met most of their friends, such as members of the Who and Thin Lizzy, and not surprisingly Villa Park and the first division seemed light years away.

One night at a party I was introduced to an American girl called Donna. At the time the craze over there was an electronic computerised game called Simon. It was shaped like a flying saucer and would light up in different colours, and you had to try to remember the various sequences of light and then match them by pressing the flying saucer. Donna and I were entranced by this game and we sat for ten hours playing against each other. When we started the music was thundering on in the background as the drink flowed freely in the Californian night and when we finished all was quiet as the sun crept over the hills. It was one of those strange and mystical moments in life you always remember; after that Donna and I went our separate ways. I didn't know who she was or where she came from but a few years later our paths crossed again in, of all places, an English television studio. I was appearing on breakfast television prior to Everton's Cup Final and among the other guests was actor John Hurt, star of such films as "Elephant Man" and "The Bob Champion Story". His American girlfriend was with him and as soon as we were introduced we recognised each other. It was Donna. Since then we've become good pals again and Donna has taken up as a football supporter. She's even travelled on the Everton team coach to Wembley and her prized soccer souvenir now is my Cup Final Shirt.

So the summer of 1979 was an enjoyable one but also a hard one as well because, apart from having the time of my life, I was trying to get back to full fitness. The Bel Air mansion had its own swimming pool which was useful both for relaxing and for training in as I pushed my body back into physical exercise. Apart from swimming I used the steep Bel Air hills as a running track and every day would push myself to the top as the sun blazed down. At first it was agony to get my right knee strong and my hosts, Black Sabbath, thought me crazy as they watched me slowly slog up the hills in the distance, as they sprawled in the heat around the pool. I knew I had to be fit and my knee needed to be back to normal for the start of a new season which would soon be on the horizon. I don't know whether it was the luxurious surroundings of Los Angeles or the Californian sun but when I got back home to Birmingham I felt pretty dejected. It's always difficult after a holiday to get back to work and even footballers, believe it or not, have been known to suffer from the Monday morning blues. When the time came to start preparing for a new season, deep down I knew that I could not face another year under the Ron Saunders regime at Villa Park.

 # THE MOVE

If I had a pound for every time a football fan has asked me why I left Aston Villa, I would be well on my way to being a millionaire by now. The move from Villa park to Molineux was one of the most controversial of my career and the transfer saga ran for weeks. Rumour has often said I moved for the money. The tale was with my night club in trouble I needed cash quickly to save myself from financial ruin. A good plot for a book or a soap opera perhaps, but I'm afraid not the truth.

I left Aston Villa for one reason – manager Ron Saunders. He was the man who had branded me a cheat and I'd never forgiven him for it. On top of that he was becoming more like a dictator than a football manager and when we started training again in July 1979 I realised that my desire to play for him was no longer there. Aston Villa was still important to me and I think I can remember saying in my first season there, once a Villa supporter always a Villa supporter and I still stand by that, but with Ron Saunders in power I could see no future for me at the club. We didn't get on and in truth after a couple of flat seasons I honestly thought my prospects would be much brighter away from him. At the time the club was going through a re-building stage and Villa's chances of achieving success looked pretty slim. After many hours of cross-examining myself I decided to ask for a transfer. I told Ron Saunders of my decision and he said there was no way he'd let me leave. I was under contract and he was determined to hold me to it. "If you say no I'll just put the request in writing and make it official," I told him. He replied, "I'll just have to rip it up then." Round one to him, but a few days later I made it known publicly I was unhappy and wanted to leave the club. The papers fell over themselves to get hold of the story and Saunders was so incensed by me talking to the press behind his back that he fined me £100. Before training one morning I grabbed hold of him and demanded, "What the hell are you playing at? I can't believe what you are saying and you dare fine me again. I'll speak to who I like." That sounding off earned me a sentence to the old leper colony, as we called it, when the Villa manager treated some his less favoured players as outcasts and made them train on their own or with the reserves. He didn't fine me again though, and in all I made three transfer requests before the Villa directors finally decided I could leave.

Before that Saunders and I crossed swords again during a pre-season trip to Scotland. Some papers ran a story about me changing my mind and deciding to stay with the club and Saunders was quoted at length. Whether it was a clever ploy on his part, wishful thinking or a misunderstanding I don't know, but it was a total fabrication and only strengthened my resolve to get away from him. For several weeks we never spoke to each other and to make matters worse for him full-back John Gidman was having a running battle as well. Like me, Giddy was not a yes man and we were looked upon, by Saunders I guess, as potential troublemakers who would not carry out his every command to the letter. On top of all this there was trouble brewing in the board room and the manager found himself in the middle of a power struggle. Over the years the club had been pulled apart by boardroom battles of one sort or another and this latest one brought another cloud over Aston Villa. To be honest, players rarely get involved in such business and although we were all well aware of the undercurrents in the boardroom it had little effect on the team. There was a suggestion, depending on which way the power battle went, that Ron Saunders might even be in danger of losing his job. It was no secret the board was split over their decision to sell John Gidman and me, and at the time there were several others unhappy at the way things were being run. On top of that the Villa supporters were openly campaigning for me to stay at the club and so the manager and the directors found themselves being pushed into a tight corner. Friction was begining to build and in the end the club had no alternative but to sell both Giddy and me. Finally, when Ron Saunders and the board accepted the transfer requests, they put a valuation on John Gidman of £750,000 and my selling price was a staggering £1 million. I was pleased to be up for sale, but the price tag, I thought, was crazy and so did a few others. The press for instance were quick to point out that after three operations on my knee and several other injury problems I was being over-valued and not many teams would be prepared to gamble so much money on a player who had to prove his fitness.

My opinion then, and it hasn't changed since, was that Ron Saunders did not really want me to leave Aston Villa. I suspect he thought by asking so much money for a player who'd been on the sidelines injured for five months he would scare buyers off, and if nobody came in with a bid, I'd have to stay with the team. What he hadn't bargained for was the crazy workings of the football transfer market. There was no shortage of speculation about which club were going to sign me but I honestly thought that unless Villa could be persuaded to drop their asking price of £1 million then I'd be spending some time in the reserves until I made my peace with the Villa manager.

The row between Ron Saunders and I was common knowledge around the club and led to one of the most amazing meetings I've ever had with football club directors. Out of the blue John Gidman and I were asked to attend a board meeting at Villa Park. We were under orders not to discuss it with anyone else especially the manager, but that was not really a problem seeing Ron Saunders and I were hardly talking at that stage. So one afternoon Giddy and I were summoned into the inner sanctum at Villa Park to face the board of directors. They wanted to know why we were so desperate to leave the club. I told them the truth: I'd lost respect for the manager and felt my ambition to win cups and competitions could be best served by moving on somewhere else. The questions came thick and fast from the board. Would I be happy with a new contract? A longer contract perhaps? Did I want more money? What could the board do to persuade me to stay? They were obviously concerned about the growing force of public opinion that I was possibly leaving Villa, which had resulted in some season ticket holders threatening not to renew their places or even rip up their book of tickets if I went. To all their questions I could only offer a negative answer and John Gidman did exactly the same. Sure, I could have asked for a longer contract and I'm certain could have negotiated more money for myself but they were not the right solutions. Then one of the directors came out with a stunning question. "Would you stay with Aston Villa if we were to get a new manager?" Giddy dived in straight away. "It might make me change my mind," he said. I couldn't help laughing at John's rush of blood, but once again I told the board it would make no difference to me. It was wrong, I thought, of the directors to undermine the club in such a way by asking a player to engage in a power struggle with the manager. No matter how much I disliked Ron Saunders then, I could not bring myself to stab the man in the back in such a cold-blooded fashion. I've often wondered what would have happened if I'd have said yes. Would they have sacrificed the manager to keep me?

By coincidence Ron Saunders was summoned to a board meeting as well, as the directors held quite an inquest into what was going on behind the scenes at Villa Park and why there was much unrest. I bet they didn't tell him what they'd asked me though! He survived that bumpy spell, of course, and went on to bring the League Championship to the club while I packed my bags and left. One comment I'd like to make before departing though, is Ron Saunders' questioning of my loyalty to Aston Villa when I decided to leave; he said I should have honoured my contract. At the time it annoyed me because I was very fond of the club, but a few years later I felt vindicated when Saunders himself left Villa Park and joined their arch rivals Birmingham City. Now if crossing the second city soccer lines like that isn't disloyal then I don't know what is. With hand on heart I can honestly say I would never play for Birmingham City for much the same reasons I could never play for Glasgow Celtic. And I must point out as well, when the chance came to go back to Villa, I jumped at the opportunity to play for the team I've always felt more for than any other.

In the summer of 1979 though, I felt the best thing for all concerned would be for me to make a move and try my luck elsewhere. I must confess when I looked to the future I was thinking in terms of Liverpool, Manchester United, one of the London clubs perhaps, or nearer home, Nottingham Forest. One of the last teams I'd given any thought to was Wolverhampton Wanderers who, under new manager John Barnwell, were beginning to build for the future.

The story behind the move to Molineux is a fascinating one in many ways because unbeknown to me it started at the end of the previous season when Aston Villa had made moves to buy Wolves midfield player Steve Daley. John Barnwell was willing to do business but Saunders wanted Wolves to give him £500,000 in cash and Daley, and in return I would go to Molineux. Wolves turned the deal down, not because they didn't want me, but because they thought they could get a better price for Daley elsewhere. The transfer went cold then, mainly because John Barnwell had a horrific car crash in which he nearly lost his life and spent the entire summer convalescing abroad. While he was in Portugal, relaxing and recovering his strength, Barnwell happened to meet up with the Manchester City's Malcolm Allison who told him they were interested in signing Daley. Now this was the sort of merry-go-round that eventually took me to Wolves for just £25,000. When he returned from abroad, John Barnwell started to press forward with his transfer plans. Villa again suggested an exchange deal with Wolves, but the two clubs couldn't agree on the price and to be honest I wasn't keen to be used as a trade for another player. I wanted to go to a club which was really interested in me. It appeared all along I was Wolves main target even though John Barnwell went down several other avenues. Apart from Villa, Everton were chasing Steve Daley who, it seemed, held the key to the whole transfer. Barnwell's next move was to set up talks with the then Goodison Park manager Gordon Lee and the initial plan was to work an exchange deal involving Daley and Bob Latchford. The England striker even had talks with Wolves and if that deal had gone through there would have been a touch of irony about it. In my first season at Dundee United Everton had wanted to sign me.

Their scout north of the border watched me for several weeks and tried hard to convince the Merseyside men I was worth a try. They were on the verge of making an offer in fact, but at the last minute decided to opt for experience and signed a number nine from Birmingham City . . . his name Bob Latchford. This time around though Latchford stayed where he was mainly because Steve Daley didn't want to go to Goodison Park.

Finally, on Sunday, September 2nd, the transfer market began to come to the boil. John Barnwell had been tipped off that Liverpool and perhaps Nottingham Forest were on the verge of joining the chase for me. Liverpool were always looking to strengthen their squad while Forest were selling centre forward Tony Woodcock to Cologne, the German side, and Barnwell reckoned Brian Clough might try to sign me as a replacement. He decided to move quickly and on that Sunday got Manchester City manager Tony Book to underwrite a £1 million bid for Daley. Barnwell rang Ron Saunders who agreed to take £1.2 million in cash for me. There was still a snag because Wolves couldn't afford the difference between the two fees. On Sunday night Barnwell forced Manchester City up to £1,150,000 in their bid for Steve Daley and then picked up the phone to offer Ron Saunders £1,175,000 for me. The bid was accepted and John Barnwell had achieved a great juggling act as I was going to cost him only £25,000. With the ten per cent signing levy and fifteen per cent V.A.T. the fee was a staggering £1,469,000.

On the Monday morning Ron Saunders called me into his office at Villa's training ground and broke the news that he'd accepted Wolves' record breaking bid. I went off to Molineux that very afternoon for my first chat with John Barnwell who impressed me right from the start with his ambitious aggression. After some lengthy talks I left Wolves and agreed to go back there again on the Wednesday for further discussions. What was worrying me most was whether joining Wolverhampton Wanderers was a step in the right direction. Despite their great tradition, Wolves hadn't achieved much in recent years, and you could hardly class them as a glamour club. Barnwell though, was a draw; he had signed Emlyn Hughes the former skipper of Liverpool and England and had several other moves up his sleeve; the club had also just built a new luxury stand and had adventurous ideas to redevelop the rest of the ground as well. So the future looked promising.

On the Wednesday I went back for more talks and apart from seeing Barnwell chatted to assistant manager Ritchie Barker, trainer Ian Ross who was at Villa when I first arrived, and also Emlyn Hughes. The "Crazy Horse," as he was known, said a lot to convince me that Wolves were a club of great promise and under Barnwell and Barker things were looking bright. Their track record, I must admit, had been promising in the first few months. Barnwell and Barker had arrived at Molineux just before Christmas the previous year and had not only rescued Wolves from relegation but steered them to an FA Cup semi-final against Arsenal. They'd lost that 2-0 but there was an air of confidence which was more than could be said of Villa at the time.

Until now money had not been discussed. It turned out later that I was not the only one who was thinking seriously about the move to Molineux. John Barnwell admitted although I was the sort of player he wanted, I had to convince him of my desire to play for the club. On the Thursday we sat down again at Molineux for yet more talks and by now the papers were full of speculation. "Gray... It's Day Two of Talks – Another Molineux Transfer Summit," was the headline in the local paper and John Barnwell appeared confident of settling the deal. "I'm prepared to make Andy Gray the most expensive player in the game because I know exactly what he can do. He's the right age, has the right attitude and, most important, he's a winner. He's achieved a lot in a short time but I believe he has only touched the edges of his potential," was the exciting fighting talk from Barnwell. On the Thursday we talked terms and considering the amount of money at stake and that this was a new British record fee, everything was settled in no time at all. With a contract and terms sorted out I left Molineux that afternoon more or less convinced I would be joining the Wolves. I told John Barnwell I was happy and subject to a few last minute details would sign for him. On the Friday morning I was back up at Bodymoor Heath, Villa's training ground which lies in the country to the north of Birmingham, for a practice session with the Villa reserves. After training I picked up my boots and said the goodbyes before leaving for my new club.

Although I thought the transfer was the right move I still felt unsure about leaving Villa. I'd been happy with the club and had enjoyed some great times. Should I stop on a little longer and give it another go I asked myself? Outside the dressing rooms a pack of pressmen were waiting for the news. I told them I had agreed to join Wolves and would be signing for them the next day. I also put the cat amongst the pigeons by telling them how John Gidman and I had been summoned to that private board meeting and had been asked to name my price to stay by the directors. It brought another flurry of headlines such as "Gray Won't Wait – Late Villa Plea Fails to Stop £1.4m Deal," and "Villa Can't Stop Gray". But as I headed for my cottage in the Staffordshire countryside I was still unsure about the future. To everyone else it was cut and dried. Villa were expecting to sell me, Wolves were planning the signing ceremony and yet here I was on the eve of the big day still in two minds. I sat at home and went through everything step by step. What were my reasons for leaving Villa Park? Were they the right ones? Why was I joining Wolves? Would my future be brighter there? It was a time of inner turmoil and the man who finally advised me and convinced me what I was doing was right was Bill Shankly – the legendary Liverpool manager. Before that week I'd only exchanged a hello or a good afternoon to him when I'd seen him at various grounds up and down the country. To a young player such as myself he was quite an awe-inspiring figure and a man who drew respect wherever he went.

Bill Shankly had been drawn quite close to Wolves. His old skipper and first mate on the Anfield ship, Emlyn Hughes, was there, of course, and he'd also become quite friendly with John Barnwell. The Wolves manager had apparently turned to Mr Shankly for guidance and advice and on that Friday night I did exactly the same. We must have been on the phone for nearly half an hour as I outlined my doubts. Bill Shankly was a good listener and his advice was that I should leave Villa and join Wolves. It was based on two things: first, he was not a great admirer of Ron Saunders' methods and came out with that great quote about his demanding training techniques and never have seen a football pitch with a one in four gradient; and secondly, he admired John Barnwell. He thought he was a young promising manager and a sincere person who would not let anyone down. Mr Shankly liked the atmosphere as well at Molineux and reckoned it was a club with a bright future. On his advice alone I decided at the eleventh hour I would sign for Wolves the next day and turn my back on Aston Villa.

The Saturday, of course, was an incredibly exciting and unforgettable day and in those first few weeks I thanked my lucky stars for listening to the advice of Bill Shankly. I made my debut for Wolves against Everton at Goodison Park the following week and scored their first goal in a 3-2 win. It was a vital goal and a vital game for me because everybody was looking to see why Wolves had paid so much money to sign a player whose career had been punctuated with injuries. The transfer fee never weighed on my shoulders during a game. It might sound a cliché, but once the referee's blown his whistle, you just concentrate on playing your game, getting a goal or two and, most important of all, winning. I couldn't have hoped for a better start to a new career, especially when you remember I'd been out injured for five months. "Anyone wanting to know what makes a footballer worth £1.5 million needed only to ask Everton's dazed and bewildered defenders after Andy Gray drove Wolves to a 3-2 victory. Skill, bravery, control, pace and a tremendous appetite for work, even after a five month lay-off, all mean that if anyone was worth that amount of money this is your man," was the verdict of the *Daily Star* newspaper. The *Daily Mail* on the other hand said, "All action Gray looks a bargain. If ever anyone looks worth £1.5 million, it's Andy Gray." It was words like these that brought my confidence flowing back and there's a tale about my Wolves debut I must tell you from Villa Park. On the same day the Villa first team were playing away and losing to Crystal Palace while the reserves were in action at Villa Park. As the second team game finished the loudspeakers announced two results: first Crystal Palace 2 Aston Villa 1 which was greeted with a groan of disappointment from the supporters; and then Everton 2 Wolves 3 . . . and yes he has scored; the crowd cheered although my name was never actually mentioned.

The first few weeks with Wolves were unbelievable in terms of results. After beating Everton we faced League leaders Manchester United at Molineux and smashed then 3-1. I scored on my home debut and again we won an avalanche of acclaim. "Super Wolf . . . Soccer's Simmering Volcano," I was called in the *Sunday Mirror* while in the *Express* it was "Gray Grabs the Goal and the Glory". The following week we did it again. At Highbury we beat Arsenal 3-2 and this time I got two. Wolves were in the top six in the first division while Villa were just three off the bottom. My move had not only been a success but it had been justified as well. I felt as though I was embarking on another of those years when everything I touched turned to gold. This time it was the old gold and black of Wolves which was emerging as the new surprise force in the first division. For me, after months of injuries, worries, tension, arguments and upsets, the sun was shining again. I was still only twenty-three and had found contentment again. I was happy with my club, the goals were going in and my knee was getting stronger with every game which was perhaps the most encouraging thing. Although I'd scored four goals in my first three games with Wolves, I knew I was not yet fully fit and looked forward with anticipation to the time when Andy Gray, the Tartan Wanderer, would be firing on all cylinders again.

10 WONDERFUL WOLVES

The Molineux years may not have matched those at Villa for personal success or compared favourably with the team triumphs at Everton, but in four full seasons with the Wolves I saw more action than most players see in a lifetime. With no fewer than four different managers, three chairmen, a League Cup win at Wembley, relegation and then promotion, there was never any shortage of excitement. On top of all that, I was nearly sold twice: first for a million pounds to Leeds United; and then for a mere £50,000 to Manchester United as the great Wolves fought for their lives aginst the harsh realities of modern day football finances. There were many who thought I was stepping out of the spotlight in the Midlands when I left Villa, but they should have known that for some reason or other the action always has a strange habit of following Andy Gray around!

That first season at Molineux was perhaps the best the Wolves have had in a long time. John Barnwell and Ritchie Barker had pulled together a more than useful side. Experience was our secret; in Emlyn Hughes, Ken Hibbitt, Willie Carr and John Richards we had four of the best professionals you're ever likely to come across. Emlyn was a natural skipper who'd won so many battles with Liverpool and England. His mere presence in the dressing room was an extra advantage and, although as a player he was nearing the end, his know-how and knowledge was priceless. Emlyn, I know, has had his critics but he always knew how to look after himself, but then in football that's so often the name of the game. He did a magnificent job for Wolves in the first season and was a true professional. Like the three other senior pros, Hibbitt, Carr and Richards, he was overjoyed with victory and hurt by defeat while one or two of the other Wolves players didn't seem to feel strongly one way or of the other. Willie Carr and Kenny Hibbitt were two great competitors. They never gave less than their all and not many other teams liked playing against them because they knew Willie and Hibby would give them a run around. John Richards, Richo, was another class player who sadly never achieved as much as his talent should have allowed him to. He could turn and strike as well as any man I've played alongside and gave the Wolves some great goals to remember him by. He was an unselfish man which made him a pleasure to play with, and in that first season our partnership brought nearly half of Wolves' total haul of goals.

The most refreshing thing about arriving at Wolves was the way everyone made me feel welcome. Although I was the big money buy, the record signing, and was attracting all the publicity, there was never any backbiting which can often happen in a dressing room. I think the mood was best summed up by Kenny Hibbitt, who on hearing the news that Wolves were signing Andy Gray rushed home to tell his wife. "If we sign Andy Gray I reckon I can bank on scoring about fifteen goals this season," he told her. And Kenny's prediction wasn't far off as Wolves began to roll along. With Barnwell and Barker in control the results kept coming, although as in many partnerships there were disagreements. Barnwell's philosophy was the same he used as a player. He liked to see the ball being knocked about and the Wolves had the players to do that. Ritchie, meanwhile, liked to tell players exactly what to do every minute of the game from the touchline. If a player is not good enough to pick the right pass though, there's nothing you can do about it.

I got on with Ritchie socially like a house on fire, but I'm afraid didn't agree with some of his football thoughts. There was a time he threatened to drop me because I wouldn't follow his orders. He wanted me to be a target man and just stand at the far post and wait for the ball. He must have realised from my Villa days that my main strength was being allowed to roam in the box and attack the ball.

The other slight niggle between Barnwell and Barker was that both wanted to be manager. Barny was still recovering from his car crash and in his absence Ritchie had run the club for several months. I'm not sure whether Ritchie could come to terms with life as a number two but despite the differences the partnership worked wonders for the Wolves. In my first season we finished up sixth in the table and might have won the championship if not for our form at home. We only managed nine League victories at Molineux and sad as it may sound most of the players enjoyed playing away more. With the building of the new stand the pitch had been moved further over and the ground was devoid of atmosphere. Only once or twice did it ever really get humming with excitement and the players certainly noticed it. Our home record was only just better than Derby County's who were relegated that season, while our away record of ten wins was bettered only by Liverpool, the champions and Arsenal, who finished two places above us in fourth spot.

Without doubt the highlight of the season was the Wembley League Cup Final against Notthingham Forest, but it was a game I nearly missed out on and was saved by, of all clubs, Aston Villa. Just before the final in March, I'd been given a one match ban after collecting twenty penalty points. I was due to serve this five days before the final, as Wolves had a League game against Villa arranged. On the Saturday though, Villa were playing at West Ham in the FA Cup and if they drew, a replay would mean the postponement of the Wolves match which in turn meant I'd miss the final through suspension. That Saturday my brother Duncan and I were at Molineux watching the reserves and as always several supporters were listening to their radios. We were desperate to follow the score from West Ham and with only a few minutes left news came it was still 0-0 and heading for a certain draw. That's it I thought, I'm going to miss the Wembley final. I felt completely dejected as I left my seat in the stand to go and watch the results coming in on the teleprinter. Suddenly a cheer went up outside and we rushed to the window. I thought the reserves had scored, but the news was even better than that. West Ham had taken the lead against Villa with only seconds to go. Ken McNaught had given away a penalty which another old Dundee United boy

Ray Stewart had scored from and if the score stayed the same it meant I would be walking out at Wembley after all. A few moments later the final score West Ham 1 Aston Villa 0 came through on the television and that was one of the few times I've ever celebrated the Villa Park men getting beaten. Funny thing is though, I told some pressmen I was going to buy Ray Stewart a crate of champagne for scoring that goal. I never did, but Ray rarely lets me forget I still owe him a glass or two. So we were all set for Wembley on the Saturday and although Nottingham Forest were favourites, we all felt we would win. You often hear a saying "Our name's on the Cup" and that year it was.

In the earlier rounds we'd luckily managed to scrape through against sides such as Grimsby and Swindon and it seemed we could do no wrong. The final itself was just the same. Forest outplayed us, but we got the only goal of the game and lifted the cup. And what a lucky goal it was – about the most fortunate winner Wembley has ever seen. Peter Daniel pumped a long ball towards the Forest box and a mix up between David Needham and Peter Shilton allowed me in to score. I take some of the credit though because, as Needham went for the ball, I could see Shilton coming off his line. Needham hadn't seen this because his eyes were fixed on the ball, so I decided not to go up to challenge, and sure enough the Forest defender chested the ball down to where he thought Shilton was waiting. I read the misunderstanding and nipped into grab the glory.

The winner at Wembley, no matter how lucky, was a goal to remember and the next day just about the whole of Wolverhampton turned out to cheer through the streets as we paraded the cup on an open top bus. It was the first time I'd been in such a parade and how marvellous it was, as the gold and black scarves filled the pavements on the way to the Town Hall. Everyone was happy and the players all thought our League Cup Final win was proof that Wolves were on the march again.

The only disappointment I had that first season at Molineux came from the Scotland team. Shortly after the League Cup Final win I'd been recalled to the national side and scored in a 4-1 win over Portugal at Hampden. At the end of the season I was picked in the squad for the home internationals and all set to lead the Scotland attack. As it turned out Wolves were playing Arsenal on the same day Scotland were due to face Northern Ireland in Belfast, and I was forced to put club before country. Arsenal were still in the running for a place in Europe and if they won their last two matches against Wolves and Middlesbrough would win a place in the UEFA cup at the expense of Ipswich Town. The Suffolk side, seeing the danger, made the League force Wolves to play their strongest side against Arsenal which meant I had to travel back to play. We lost 2-1, I got injured and that made me miss Scotland's next game against Wales. However, I was promised a place in the side against England at Hampden and had phoned my family to tell them the good news. I'd never played against England in a full international and was desperately looking forward to it. On the Friday before the big match there was disappointment when Scotland manager Jock Stein pulled me aside in training to tell me he was playing Joe Jordan instead and I was to be one of the substitutes. What a sickener that was and further proof of my international career being dogged with bad luck. As I sat on the bench at Hampden and watched Scotland struggle I could hear the fans chanting my name and when I did get a chance to go on late in the match, it was really too late, England were winning 2-0. The whole irony is that Arsenal never did make it to Europe because they lost to Middlesbrough in their final game, but it cost me another couple of caps and a real chance to have a crack at the soccer sassenachs.

Back at Molineux times were changing, sadly for the worse, and little did anyone realise it but the big Wolves decline was underway. Everyone knew at the end of the League Cup winning season that the team needed fresh blood. Time was catching up on players like Emlyn Hughes, Derek Parkin and Willie Carr, and it was vital to get some new players to keep us on top. John Barnwell went down the right avenues and chased players like Peter Reid, who was then at Bolton. Peter even came to watch us one Saturday but Wolves' financial troubles were beginning to bite, and there was not enough money in the kitty to buy the quality we needed. That was the turning point in my book. Had Wolves stuck their necks out and borrowed to buy, the club could have achieved great things. I believe John Barnwell was capable of leading the team to a League Championship or an FA Cup win but with the limited resources he had there was only one way . . . and that was down.

We started the 1980-81 season disastrously. After losing five of our first eight matches and suffering a humiliating League Cup defeat at the hands of Cambridge United, we then fell at the first hurdle in the UEFA Cup against PSV Eindhoven. Come October the season already looked pretty bleak; we were in the bottom half of the table with only the FA Cup to look forward to. Charged by Barny's enthusiasm we put together a run which took us through to the semi-finals against Spurs at Hillsborough. It was a great game to play in but with just minutes to go we were 2-1 down. Kenny Hibbitt was then tripped in the box and Willie Carr hit the equaliser from the penalty spot. In extra time we murdered Tottenham but the winning goal just wouldn't come and the final whistle brought more than the end of the game. It was the end of a great run under John Barnwell. We lost the replay 3-0 and although Barny stayed on as manager until the following New Year things were never the same again.

Ritchie Barker left us to take charge of Stoke City and the Wolves financial crisis began to grow. It was so bad that at the start of the following season the club tried to sell me to raise much needed money. And it says a lot when I tell you Wolves could have accepted a bid of £900,000 in cash from Leeds United for me. The Molineux directors wanted £1 million and they wouldn't budge. In hindsight, a deal then might have helped save the club from the awful arrival of the debt collectors. John Barnwell didn't want to sell me but knew the only way to raise cash to strengthen his team was to let me go. Leeds were keen and willing to pay, as I say, £900,000 and I would have gone. The deal hung in the balance for weeks until finally Leeds got fed up of waiting and pulled out. It left Wolves with no money for new players and by Christmas the alarm bells were ringing. We were just off the bottom of the table and there was war between John Barnwell and the board. It ended inevitably with Barny resigning and that led to ugly demonstrations against chairman Harry Marshall and his directors. At one match irate fans even staged a sit-in on the pitch and everyone felt the club was slowly rotting away.

I was sorry to see Barny go because he was such a lively and loveable figure. Even in the dark days he had a joke and a smile for everyone and could lift any dressing room. The only sad thing was I don't think I ever saw the best of him. Those who knew him well before his car crash reckoned he never fully recovered from his frightful injuries. He used to get tired quickly and if not for the car crash and the club's financial trouble I believe John Barnwell could have done great things for Wolverhampton Wanderers. Only now is he perhaps fully recovered and there are a few clubs who could do a lot worse than give him another go. But, to use one of Barny's own favourite sayings, "As one door closes, another opens," and his place at Molineux was taken by another capable and well respected manager in Ian Greaves.

Ian Greaves had done duty with Huddersfield, and Bolton in the first division, and was a man I took to straight away. Sadly we were too deep in trouble by the time he came and, although we got on well, it was Ian Greaves who gave me one of the biggest verbal batterings I've ever had. That season was a bad one for me for behaviour. In September I'd been sent off for only the second time in my career against Villa of all sides. It came in a League Cup match in my first game back at Villa Park as a Wolves player. You can imagine the kind of welcome I got as I ran out in the Wolves shirt: "Villa reject," they shouted, but by half-time they were eating their words as Wolves went in 1-0 up thanks to an Andy Gray goal. In the second half though, it was their turn to gloat as I was sent off for a silly tackle on the Villa skipper Dennis Mortimer. Looking back it was something I regretted as soon as it happened. Whenever I got into trouble the whole team seemed to suffer. Dennis and I had never been the best of friends at Villa. As captain he was close to Ron Saunders and sided with him when the rows broke out, but that was no excuse for what I did. For no reason I lost my head for a few seconds and went for him after the ball had gone. From the stands it looked a deadly challenge; I was all of twenty-five minutes too late in going in. I suppose it was nasty because I did have a crack at him and if I'd connected would have hurt him. Luckily I never actually made contact and the challenge looked far worse than it actually was. The referee, Clive White, was over in a second and with no hesitation sent me off. I think he reacted strongly and might have been influenced by the crowd who were calling for my blood, but I could hardly argue. It was a disastrous return to Villa Park. As I ran off it seemed the whole ground was sneering at me and I was angry with myself for losing control. When I left Wolves were two up but Villa came back to win 3-2 and you could put that defeat down to my temper.

The other sending-off which landed me in hot water with Ian Greaves came at Stoke towards the end of the season. Both teams were fighting off relegation and it was a match we both needed to win. Subsequently there was a lot of tension and bad tempers and I blew it again by getting sent off for arguing. The referee awarded a penalty against Wolves and two or three of us went in to protest against his decision. For some reason he picked me out and sent me off for dissent. Wolves lost 2-1 and afterwards Ian Greaves accused me of throwing away Wolves first division future. "Getting sent off has cost us the first division," he said in the dressing room as he blew his top and tore into me. His language was ripe at the best of times and that afternoon he must have used every four letter word he could think of as he gave me the biggest dressing down I've ever had. I couldn't defend myself even though I thought I'd been hard done by. Sure enough I was suspended and Wolves did go down, and I suppose it's incidents like that which have earned me a troublemaker tag.

I've only been sent off three times, once for Scotland and then twice in that season with Wolves. Usually it's my mouth which has landed me in trouble. I know I talk too much but that's part of my make-up and the mate who reckons they designed the instamatic camera in order to get a picture of me with my mouth shut wasn't far wrong. For a time I became a marked man and I think some referees are influenced by players' reputations. Most should know that from time to time I blow my top but after letting off steam it's all forgotton. That's why I was glad to see the back of the red and yellow cards as they made it too easy for the referee to book someone or send somebody off. If he's got to call a player to him and then get out his book, both the referee and the player have had an extra few vital seconds to cool down.

One of my favourite referees was the old Welsh wizard Clive Thomas who also made a few enemies. I liked him because he would always make a decision and stand by it. Too many referees take the easy way out and let things go, but Clive was a man of decision who had the gift of spotting incidents off the ball as well. The referee of last season's Cup Final, Peter Willis, took a lot of hammering for sending off Kevin Moran. He had a poor game, I think, but I respect him for being brave to make a positive decision which he thought was right and then sticking to it. The funniest clash I had with a referee came against Clive Thomas. I was playing for Villa at the time and was annoyed by something he'd blown for. Running towards him I was waving my arms in protest and I know some refs who would have booked me or even sent me off there and then. Not Clive. He took hold of my arm and said "Look Andy, for Christ's sake don't wave your arms about. If you do that everyone in the ground can see you're having a go at me and it looks bad. As long as you keep your arms by your side you can call me what you like because the crowd don't know what you're saying." So I gave Clive a right mouthful and told him what I thought with my arms tucked tightly by me side. Clive answered me back, in the same language, and I suppose put politely you could say we had a frank exchange of views. Clive gave as good as he got, but was a top class referee. I think he'd admit it himself he was a little too book happy when he started, but in later years he mellowed and I for one was sorry to see him retire.

Back at the Wolves, meanwhile, there was turmoil of a different nature. We had been relegated but worse was to come when the club slipped into the hands of the receiver. The old board had resigned and an old friend and ally from Villa days, Doug Ellis, arrived as chairman but only for a couple of weeks. The writing was on the wall by then and Doug had no option but to call in the liquidator. Wolves were deep in debt and it seemed heading for the scrapheap. All the players were naturally concerned for both the club and themselves and amazingly, on the day Wolves were saved, I nearly became a Manchester United player. The liquidator was seriously considering accepting a bid of only £50,000 for me from Manchester United. Old Trafford manager Ron Atkinson had spotted the opportunity to cash in and at first I felt like a bit of furniture that was being sold off cheap in a closing down sale. Mind you, the thought of playing for United was an attractive one and the day before Wolves were due to go bust he phoned me to say a deal had been struck and a medical was being arranged at Old Trafford. The next day I waited by the phone and when it finally rang it brought news of a takeover at Molineux by Derek Dougan whose first decision was to turn down United's bid.

The Wolves fans looked upon Doog as a saviour, a knight in shining armour coming to the rescue on his charger with seconds to spare. And I believe they have a lot to be thankful for. The Doog was a big man with a big ego who loved being the centre of attention. He worshipped the Wolves, though, and all he wanted was to see the club successful again. Derek would work from eight o'clock in the morning until eight o'clock at night six days a week and did a great job in trying to rebuild a troubled club. He faced one big problem. The Bhatti brothers, who had supplied the cash to save Wolves, were not really interested in the football club. They saw it as seven acres of prime building land in the centre of Wolverhampton which they could develop and make a fortune. The fact that there was a famous football club fighting for its life was by the way. It became clear from very early on that although the brothers had saved Wolves, the club would have to generate its own money in order to survive and there would be no subsidies from the owners.

The brothers turned up at Molineux quite a few times in the first season and mixed freely with the players after the matches. They both appeared to be pleasant young businessmen, but their knowledge of football was very limited. It was left to Doog as chief executive to run the club and the first thing he did was to boost the wages. Now in recent months, as Wolves have hit financial problems again, Doog has taken a lot of stick for overspending. He pursued a pay policy which was initiated by John Barnwell. When I arrived at Molineux some of the players there were amongst the worst paid in the country and all Barny and Doog were trying to do was to up the wages in the hope of attracting better players. If you pay nothing you get rubbish and both Doog and Barny had ambitions to see Wolves back with the best.

I believe the real damage at Molineux was done by the building of a new luxury stand. It was more than the club could afford and destroyed the atmosphere as well. Some people believe my record signing landed Wolves in financial trouble but, as I explained a little earlier, if you take the Steve Daley transfer into consideration I only cost Wolves £25,000. That new stand cost £2.5 million and it could well turn out to be a tombstone to a once legendary club. I think it's only been filled once and the decision to build the stand must go down as one of the worst ever made in football. Supporters, I know, must be looked after, but fans would rather stand on a slagheap in the rain to watch quality than sit in comfort and endure failure. Apart from breaking Wolves at the bank the new stand also destroyed the air of excitement and enjoyment felt by so many great teams in the past. Before they redeveloped the ground Molineux was a wonderful stadium. With the stands hugging the touchline it generated a marvellous atmosphere and not many sides enjoyed running out to play there. But the new stand finished all that and even the Wolves players found it difficult to motivate themselves in the new surroundings. The pitch was too far from the crowd and at times you could have been playing in the middle of a park for all the atmosphere you got. Some, of course, reckon Wolves should have been allowed to go to the wall, as a kind of sacrificial lamb, to warn other teams of the perils of overspending. I hope things never get that bad because for so many Wolverhampton Wanderers is more than just a football club. It's part of our soccer heritage and without doubt is still the hub of the town. The fans may not go as often as they did but there's still massive support for the team and if you took that away a big part of Wolverhampton would die.

Derek Dougan, I know, did the best he could to bring success to Wolves, and it was because of him I stayed with the club for as long as I did. I'm sure I could have got a move if I wanted, but pledged my support to the team because I thought Doog was a man worth working for. We only ever had one argument and that came at the end of the first match when we had beaten Blackburn Rovers. In true Doog fashion he marched into the dressing room after the game and started cracking open bottles of champagne. I turned down his offer of a drink and told him it was wrong to start celebrating after just one match. "Listen Doog," I said, "if we win promotion, then at the end of the season I'll be the first to raise a glass." And so I was as Wolves finished in second place to jump back into the first division.

We'd been taken there by Graham Hawkins who'd replaced Ian Greaves as manager shortly after Doog took over. Sadly Greaves and the Doog had clashed in the past and there was no way they were going to work together. When Graham Hawkins arrived he was an unknown, untried manager and was handed an unenviable task, but results speak for themselves as he led the team straight back into the first division. A lot of people outside the club thought of Hawkins as Dougan's puppet, an unfair judgement because, as far as I'm concerned, the manager was always in charge. The only time the Doog used his weight as chief executive and chairman was when he signed Tony Towner from Rotherham. Doog, who'd been working for Yorkshire television as a soccer pundit, rated Towner and went in and bought him one day without consulting Graham Hawkins. That was the only time I saw the manager out-manoeuvred.

Poor old Tony Towner must have wished he'd stayed up north. Not long after joining the club he got mixed up in one of the most bizarre incidents I've ever known and suffered at the hands of mad Billy Kellock. Now Billy was one of soccer's real wanderers. Like me he was from Glasgow and had started as a kid with Aston Villa. He arrived at Molineux via Cardiff, Norwich, Milwall, Chelmsford, Kettering, Peterborough and Luton – some journey and it's not hard to see why he never stopped long in the same place. Billy was a super lad, but accident prone, football's Frank Spencer if you like, who could always be relied upon to put his foot in it. He was far from being the best player in the world, but Billy was a trier, a big-hearted individual. It was on a pre-season tour of Sweden that mad Billy made his mark. We'd been out for a few drinks and it must have been one o'clock in the morning when Billy came knocking at my hotel room door. I was sharing a room with Ken Hibbitt who got up, opened the door to find Billy standing there. Billy was sharing the room next door with Tony Towner. "What the hell's up with you Billy at this time in the morning?" asked Ken who like me was none too thrilled at being woken up. "It's Tony," said Billy. "I've smashed him in the face. I can't believe it." "Don't be so stupid Billy," said Ken. "It's true," said Billy, "Come and have a look." And so Ken and I dashed into the room next door to find Tony Towner lying on his bed as white as one of the sheets, with a great big gash over his eye. Blood was pouring from the wound and Tony was mopping it up with a towel which by now had turned deep crimson. Ken and I looked at each other and then stared hard at Billy, looking for some sort of explanation. Apparently Billy had gone into the room and not wanting to disturb Tony who was in bed had stumbled around in the dark. For some crazy reason Billy had picked up one of the metal chairs in the room and pretended to throw it through the window. Poor old Tony had stirred and sat up in bed only to be whacked in the face accidentally by mad Billy with his chair throwing routine. It took Tony days to get over the shock and as for Billy he got a right rollicking from the manager who thought him to be a bit of a troublemaker. Mad Billy was harmless really, but just one of life's unlucky souls who always seemed to land in hot water. He was a good lad to have in the team though and played his part in Wolves promotion drive.

I must admit I didn't really enjoy my one and only season in the second division. It was hard to get motivated some weeks and I found myself looking at the first division fixtures most Saturdays wishing I could be at Anfield or Old Trafford rather than Grimsby or Carlisle. I knocked in ten goals though and enjoyed my best run for sometime in the Scotland side, finally managing to get a game against England at Wembley. We lost 2-0 but at least I can stake a claim to history; unless the football authorities change their minds in the future that England v Scotland game is the last ever played at Wembley in the home internationals. For me it was the first and last, but I can always say I was there.

Sadly the great Wolves revival didn't last long. Within a few weeks of the new season we were back in trouble. We had a dream start as well; on the opening day of the season we held the champions Liverpool to a 1-1 draw. The champagne corks were popping again but the bubbles soon burst as the season went flat. In our first twelve matches we lost nine and drew three and were firmly anchored to the bottom. Relegation even at that early stage looked inevitable, so when the opportunity came to move to Everton I can honestly say I jumped at the chance to taste the soccer delights of Goodison.

11 HOME SWEET HOME

Lucky in life – lucky in love is what they always say and like all good stories my home life has a happy ending.

I don't know what it is about the name of Andy Gray but wherever I've been and whatever I've done on or off the soccer pitch the headline hunters have never been far behind. And like my soccer career I've surely had more ups and downs than most. Eight homes in ten years, a broken marriage, a kidnap threat and pages of muck raking newspaper stories are all behind me now as I settle myself for the future with my lovely lady Jan and daughter Amy.

There've been some turbulent but tremendous times and at the end of it all I would like to think I'm basically a lad from Drumchapel at heart who was lucky to score a few goals and win a few fans on the football field. I'm sure because of the publicity I've had over the years some must think of me as a wild, extravagant playboy figure. Undeniably I've enjoyed life but my football has never suffered and I've always been able to discipline myself and keep to a strict code of conduct. Discipline was all part of my upbringing. Our grandparents and our Mum made sure we all behaved ourselves as we were taught the meaning of the word respect.

My Grandpa was one of the early powerful figures in my life. He was a lovable man but a dominant one – he who must be obeyed. My grandparents lived on the Isle of Lewis, of course, where we used to spend the summer holidays and where I was always on my best behaviour. They were strict Church of Scotland folk who went to the local kirk three times a week: twice on a Sunday and once on Thursday. It was the Sundays I remember, for we were not allowed to do anything. You could not read, run, play or listen to the radio. It was a day for meditation and after Sunday lunch the villagers would take a stroll down to the local beach where everyone would gather for a walk and some gentle conversation.

As a teenager it was hard to survive and I must admit I cheated a little. On Sunday Grandma and Grandpa would cross the road to the kirk for the evening service. I usually stayed behind on my own because the services were all held in Gaelic and it was difficult for me to follow what was going on. From my grandparents' house you could see the church and as soon as they went inside I'd switch on the radio and tune it into the weekly Pick of the Pops show. On Sunday listening to the radio, especially pop music, was a sin in the eyes of the church and I had to be careful I never got caught. I'd sit in a chair listening to the top ten with an eye on the church doors. When they opened I knew it would be fifteen minutes before the service finished; you could set your watch by it. I knew as well it would take my grandparents about five minutes to make their way out of church, exchange a few pleasantries and cross the road for home. But as soon as those doors opened I had to switch the radio off. My Grandpa may have been an island man but he was no fool. The first thing he did on a Sunday night when he came in from church was to walk across to the old radio and lay his hand on top of it to feel if it was warm. He would look at me and say "I hope you've not been listening to the radio while we've been at church Andrew." "Course not Grandpa," I'd say hoping desperately the radio had cooled down enough. I'm sure he knew what I'd done and Grandpa was not a man to cross.

I can remember one holiday I travelled to Lewis with John Keir, a pal of mine from Glasgow. I'd promised him a few days on the island where we could set off and enjoy some adventures. We travelled by the usual route, by train from Glasgow and then took the steamer to Stornaway. After twelve hours we were both tired, and by the time the boat docked we were looking forward to a good meal and a long sleep. The only snag was I hadn't told my Grandpa, who was now on his own as Grandma had died, that I was bringing a friend. It might sound daft now but even though I was fourteen at the time I didn't have the courage to ask him. So, as we walked up the road to my Grandpa's house, we stopped at an old derelict cottage which had been empty for years. There was no roof on it and most of the windows were broken. I had to break the news to John that I hadn't asked my Grandpa if he could stay, and persuaded John to stop in the house while I went on ahead. Of course, when I got to Grandpa's I was still too scared to ask him and so crept out with a blanket, a pillow and some bread and made for the old house. "Do you mind stopping here the night John?" I said to my pal. "It's great here, really exciting and I'll come down first thing in the morning with some breakfast." Poor old John was a little upset. He'd come on a promise of an island holiday only to find himself camping out in a derelict cottage. Reluctantly he agreed on the proviso he would get a bed in Grandpa's house the next night. "Yes, of course, no problem. I'll ask Grandpa tonight when we're together. He won't mind – I'll tell him you're arriving on the steamer tomorrow." And that night I left John in his makeshift hotel and ran back to the village. I was fast asleep in bed when suddenly I was wakened by some strange noises from outside. Pulling myself out from under the covers I looked at the time. It was nearly three o'clock in the morning. Outside it was raining and I could hear a sort of banging noise. I jumped up and peered out of the window. Below was my mate John, who was standing in the garden throwing stones up at the window next to mine. It was the wrong window, of course, and terrified he'd wake Grandpa I shouted down to him. "What are you doing John, what's up?" "Oh Andy, am I glad to see you. It's been chucking it down with rain and I'm scared. I reckon that old cottage must be haunted or something. There's some funny noises down there. Please let me in," he cried. I've never seen a sadder face in all my days and I crept downstairs to let him in. He was soaked to the skin and trembling either from the cold or fear or perhaps both as I took him to my room. He spent the rest of the night there and in the morning I hid him in the wardrobe as the home help came in to clean for Grandpa. After breakfast they both went out and I smuggled John downstairs to give him some food. I hadn't asked Grandpa, of course, and so John reckoned it was best if he went off home to Glasgow. "I'm not staying here if there's no bed for the night Andy," he said as I saw him off on the morning steamer from Stornaway. That shows you, I suppose, how keen I was to keep out of trouble, and nothing has really changed all that much.

I was young and naive when I came down to England but found my feet with the help of some good friends. For the first few months I stopped in a local hotel in Sutton Coldfield where John Burridge, the goalie, looked after me, and then moved in with full-back John Gidman and his wife Claire. She was a saint to put up with us both. Finally I bought a little semi of my own. Aston Villa encouraged players to invest their wages by taking out a mortgage, and my next good move was to take in two lodgers, brother Duncan and my Glasgow mate Rab Jackson. We got on together like a house on fire, and without those two life would have been much harder. They made sure my feet stayed on the ground and although we enjoyed ourselves we kept to the straight and narrow. When Arsenal's Charlie Nicholas came south I gave him one bit of advice, to bring a couple of mates with him as companions if you like. A young Scots lad in a big English city can easily be led astray and I'm not sure whether Charlie ever took my advice!

Back in Brum though, Duncan, Rab and I survived quite well. I was head cook, Rab was in charge of washing-up, Duncan dried and we shared the dusting and vacuuming between us. At first I experimented over the stove and Rab or Duncs might tell you all my early meals were errors and a trial to eat, but before very long I was serving up some tasty dishes. My favourite, or rather speciality, was chilli con carne and after a time Duncan and Rab grew tired of it. Because I could cook it well we used to have it three of four times a week and whenever Duncs or Rab would ask what was for dinner invariably three voices would simultaneously say "chilli con carne". Mind you, if I hadn't learned to cook, goodness knows what would have happened to us. One day I was out and rang Rab at home to ask him to put the potatoes on. They were peeled and all Rab had to do was put a pinch of salt in and light the stove. Rab was no chef and he spent the next ten minutes or so phoning around friends for advice. Finally he got through to Villa player Alex Cropley's girlfriend and in a worried voice asked her, "I'm in a bit of a mess. Andy's asked me to put the potatoes on for dinner and I forgot to ask him something. How much salt do you put in the pan for three people," was Rab's hilarious question.

Another laugh with Rab came at the posh Midland Hotel in Birmingham. I'd been invited to a promotional evening there which was something to do with Trevor Francis who was then playing at Birmingham City. Everyone was smartly dressed and the highlight of the evening was a splendid dinner in the hotel's dining room. Good old Rab came as my guest and eating out for two batchelors was something of a treat. The first course was King Prawns, one of my favourites. When everyone on the table had been served I set to work cracking off the heads and peeling off the shell and at the same time was chatting to the person next to me. Suddenly I felt Rab, who was sitting on the other side, tugging on my sleeve. I turned and took one look at Rab who had a mouthful of prawns. "I don't think much of these Andy, they're a bit bloody crunchy!" Rab had bits of head, the spikes and shell sticking out of the corners of his mouth. He'd never had fresh prawns before and had merrily picked the first one up and bunged the whole lot into his mouth, head and all. I laughed at him but it was easily done, of course. I can remember when I first started eating out at hotels with teams and was confronted with new dishes and a complete set of cutlery. Fortunately, I had the nouse to watch everyone else before taking the plunge, and so I learnt like that.

After a short time in our little semi I bought a big new house on a development not far away. In those days it was quite a luxurious house, or as the press liked to call it, an executive home. It was like being back in Scotland because all the roads were named after golf courses. There was Troon, St. Andrews, and where we were was called Gleneagles, so the new Gray residence quickly became known as the Gleneagles Hotel. It was open house to all my mates who needed a bed for the night. Goodness knows how many we had stopping there sometimes and I reckon the neighbours were glad to see the back of me after a Christmas party to beat all parties. All the Villa players, their wives and girlfriends and the rest of the staff had been enjoying the club's annual party at the ground. Like an idiot I insisted on asking everyone back to my place for a nightcap. We had twenty cars and a seventy seater coach parked in the road and every room was full to overflowing – they were even in the garden and standing on the front lawn in the middle of December.

Being a footballer opens all sorts of doors socially. We used to enjoy our nights out at the clubs but caution was always the rule. Girls would throw themselves at you and there was always someone willing to pick an argument or a fight. I stayed out of trouble because I knew how much damage could be caused by getting involved. Only once, up in Dundee, have I ever got mixed up in a fight and then it was a case of being picked on. The secret is really knowing where to draw the line. You must enjoy yourself in life but everything, as they say, in moderation.

As far as the girls went, I had a steady date up in Scotland; a girl called Janet Ramsey was my first love back in Glasgow, but we drifted apart when I moved to Aston Villa. I was engaged to another girl very briefly before taking up with a lady called Vanessa Crosland-Taylor. We met through friends and after a time moved in with each other and went to live in a little cottage in the village of Whittington near Lichfield. It was the first major relationship I had had, and for a time everything ran smoothly. Together we overcame a kidnap threat which came shortly after I'd moved to Wolves. The papers had been full of the transfer story, and then, of course, at just under £1.5 million it was a British record. I'm sure people thought I was rolling in cash and that's what led to the kidnap drama.

I was stunned when the police called one day with news of a letter they'd received containing an anonymous tip-off. It claimed a group of men were planning to kidnap Vanessa and hold her to ransom. Apparently the chap who'd sent the letter was part of the gang but had quarrelled with the others and fallen out with them. He was getting his own back by tipping off the police. To be honest I found the story a little far fetched. Vanessa though was obviously concerned and so too were the police. They took the threatening letter very seriously and decided it merited some action, so for two or three weeks Vanessa was given a police guard. The whole thing was kept secret but it was difficult to concentrate on football with all this going on in the background. It was eerie as well, especially at night. Our cottage was set deep in the Staffordshire countryside and at night when drawing the curtains you'd look out to see a policeman on watch. Every bump or strange noise made us shiver and we were relieved when the police finally blew the all clear.

Shortly afterwards Vanessa and I got married in secret at the local registry office. My old Villa mate Alex Cropley and his girlfriend acted as witnesses and I told no one not even my Mum or brothers for months. Why? I don't know. At the time Vanessa and I wanted to be on our own and the secret of our marriage only came out when a local newspaper went digging into the marriage records at the local registry office. They must have been informed because they knew where to look and discovered the record of our marriage. The paper very kindly shared our secret with all its readers and then Fleet Street jumped on the bandwaggon demanding pictures and interviews. Vanessa and I moved home again to a little village near Wolverhampton but sadly our marriage didn't last above a year. I think we both realised in the end we weren't right for each other and so we drifted apart. To be honest I was never any good at personal relationships and I know I'm not the easiest man in the world to live with. Vanessa went to live in London and I kept the cottage and reverted to being a batchelor.

Not long after we split up a very special lady came into my life and sure enough it wasn't long before the press were hot on our heels. I was out for a night at a club in Birmingham and got talking to a girl who was there with eleven of her mates celebrating a birthday. Although I spent most of the evening with the girl, I was more taken by her friend Janet whose birthday they were celebrating. Being a gentleman to the very end I couldn't hurt my partner's feelings by chatting up her friend so I suggested we make up a foursome for another night out. I told the girl I had a friend so if she gave me Janet's number I could pass it on and we'd fix something up for the future. It was a lie, of course, because the next day I phoned Janet myself and that was the start of the best thing ever to happen to me. Janet was a nursery nurse from Birmingham. Things were difficult for her at first because I was still married to Vanessa, although we were separated. The next couple of years were among the most happy of my life. In Janet I'd found an ideal partner and our lives were enhanced with the news that our first baby was on the way. But as always, there was still unexpected trouble around the corner. Before Amy was born our life was rocked by Vanessa who got involved with some so-called pop star and the rather sordid story of their life together was splashed across the pages of the *Sun*. It wasn't very pleasant and I thought very unnecessary. Surely there must have been better things to write about than the ex-wife of Andy Gray having an affair with some chap. I kept out of it and refused to comment on the stories, although pressmen chased me for quotes. As far as I was concerned Vanessa's life was her own. I was more worried about Jan and one of the happiest days of my life was when little Amy was born.

My life was now complete, and what a lovely day it was when Jan and Amy came home to the cottage. Within weeks, though, our new life was being splashed on the front pages of the papers as reporters and photographers from London converged on the village to snatch pictures and get stories of Andy Gray's love child. The story about Amy broke in the local Wolverhampton paper, the *Express* and *Star*. They'd been digging into my life ever since the story about Vanessa and this time in my opinion they plumbed new depths. Once again they made an intense search at the local records office and came across Amy's birth certificate which had my address on it. The very next night they printed a copy of the birth certificate on the front page of the paper and suddenly the alarm bells were ringing in Fleet Street. For some crazy reason the story of a soccer player's love child seemed to drag in reporters like bees round a honey pot and the next day we were under siege. The phone never stopped ringing and photographers camped on our doorstep. For Janet the next few days were a nightmare. We had to keep the curtains closed to stop photographers trying to snatch a picture of Amy and

BOB THOMAS

DEREK MILLWARD

ABOVE *With Ritchie Barker at Wolves shortly after my £1.5 million move . . . and*

BELOW *Emlyn Hughes after our victory in the League Cup over Nottingham Forest, 1979-80.*

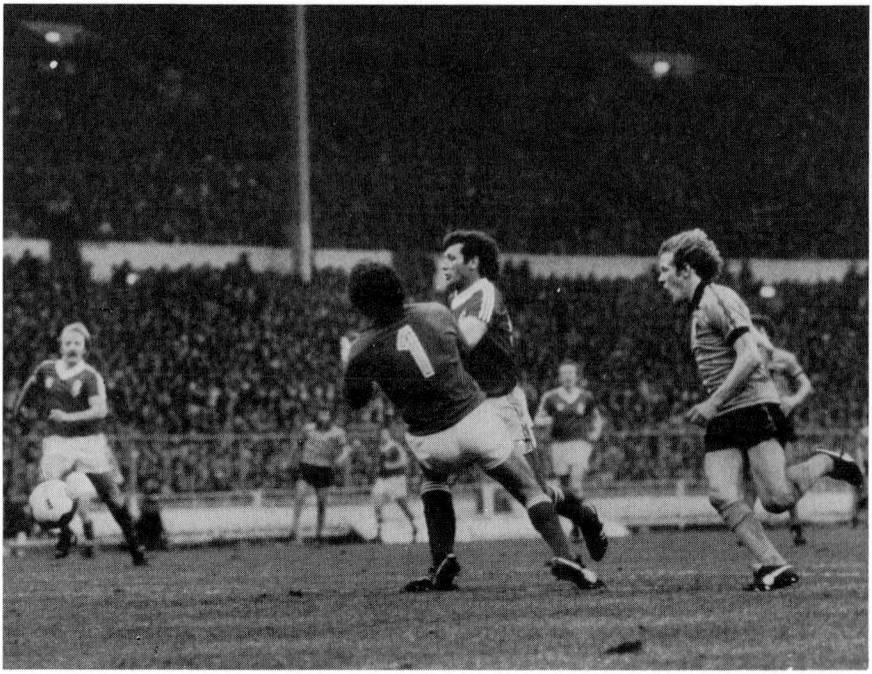

COLORSPORT

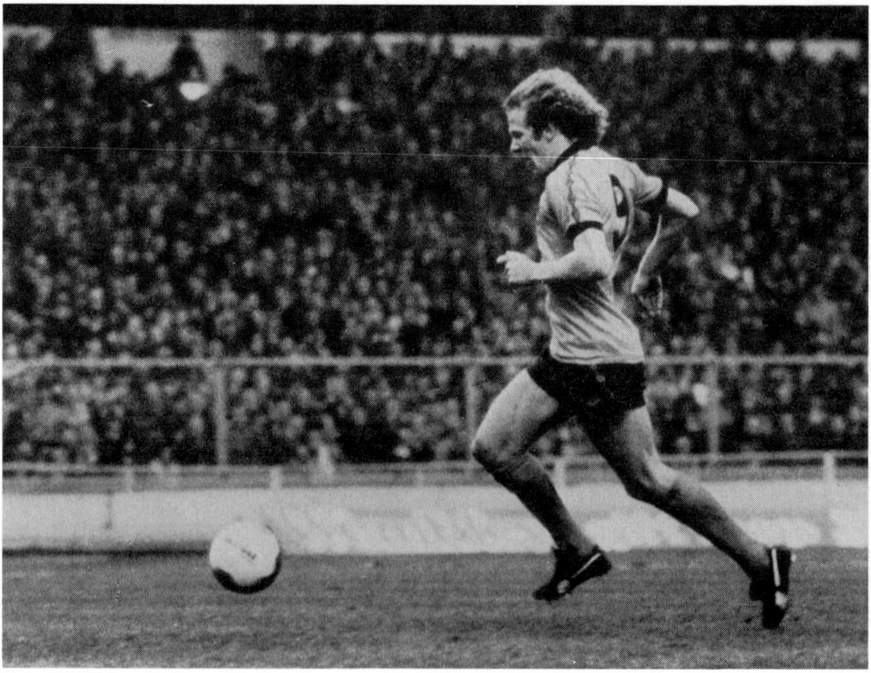

COLORSPORT

ABOVE Wolves v Notts Forest, League Cup Final, 1980. *The Mistake.*

BELOW *The realisation of what I'm about to do.*

ABOVE *The Completion.*

BELOW *Oh, what joy! The winner at Wembley.*

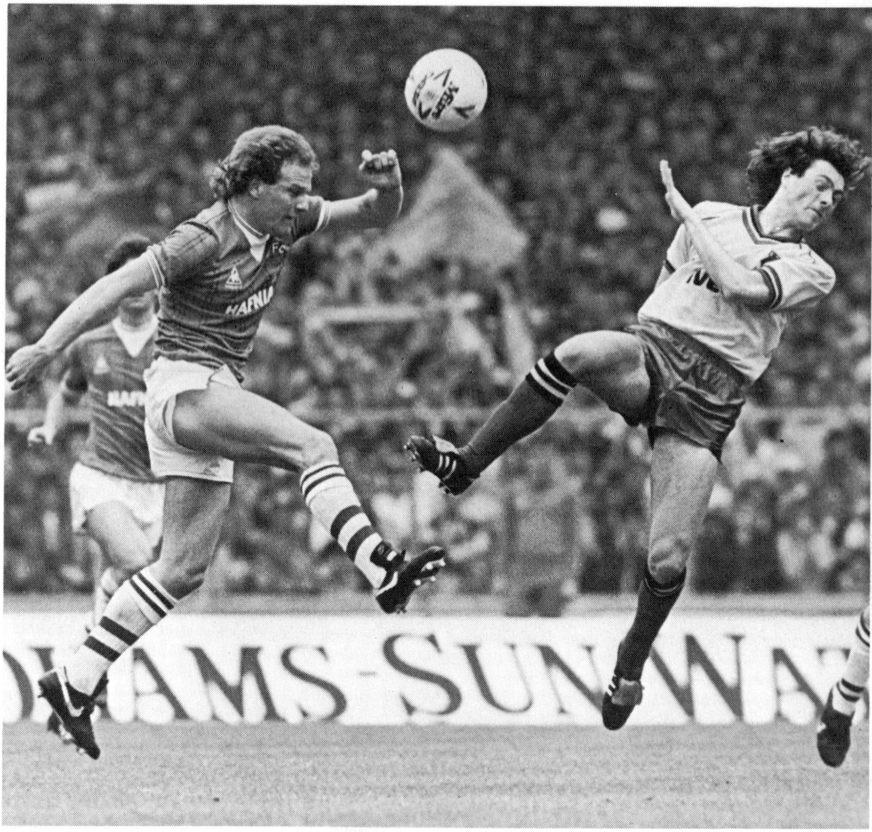

BOB THOMAS

ABOVE *My first FA Cup Final v Watford, 1984.*

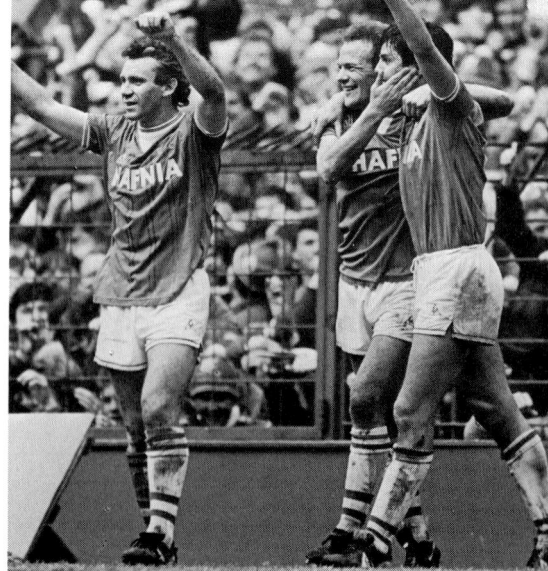

RIGHT *With two great team-mates, Peter Reid and Graeme Sharp, celebrating our 2-0 win over QPR and the realisation that Everton were League Champions, 1985.*

ABOVE FA Cup Final v Manchester United, 1985. *A typical Andy Gray challenge for a 50-50 ball.*

BELOW *"Who me Ref?" My tongue gets me in more trouble than anything.*

ABOVE *A very happy and proud lad when with the Scotland squad.*

RIGHT *One of my hardest opponents, Dave Watson.* Scotland v England, 1981.

OPPOSITE PAGE, TOP *FA Cup, 1984: a victorious Everton and the beginning of a new era.*

CENTRE *League Trophy, 1985: after twelve years I got my hands on the League Championship with the best team I've ever played in.*

BOTTOM *The second part of our double: the European Cup Winners Cup, and Everton's first European trophy, with Graeme Sharp, Kevin Sheedy and Trevor Steven.*

BOB THOMAS

I will learn to ride a tackle one of these days!

some even crept into the fields at the back of our house hoping to get the picture they wanted with long range lenses. Janet was a prisoner in her own house and the worst came when I left for training in the mornings. The press lads would watch me leave and then as soon as I was out of the drive they'd move in. The phone would ring and they'd knock at the door trying to persuade Jan to let them in. They tried to be very subtle of course, taking the line that if they could have a picture of us with Amy we'd be left in peace. There was no way I'd do that and the affair came to a head one morning when Jan finally cracked under the pressure. Again there were a pack of pressmen outside and she suddenly snapped. She phoned Wolves' training ground in a panic and cried for help. I was dragged off the pitch and coach Jim Barron lent me his car. Still in my boots and playing gear I roared off towards home, my blood boiling.

Our cottage was at the end of a narrow country lane and I raced down there like never before. As I turned the corner a car was coming the other way. My foot slammed down hard on the brakes, my hands wrenched at the wheel but the next thing I knew there was an alarming bang and the sound of breaking glass and crumpling metal. I'd crashed head on into the other car. I pulled myself out from behind the wheel and surveyed the damage. Fortunately the poor chap I'd collided with was OK but I felt the warm trickle of blood running down my face. I'd cut myself on the head and within minutes an ambulance was on the scene. By now the pressmen who'd been harrassing Jan had got wind of the crash, but luckily the ambulance boys got me in the back before they got there. On went the blue light and the siren and away sped the ambulance with the press cars chasing behind. Although I wasn't seriously injured the ambulance men realised what was going on and managed to lose them as they roared through a couple of red lights. At the hospital I had thirteen stitches in a head wound but I knew I was lucky to be alive. Had the other vehicle been going faster or had it been a lorry or a heavy vehicle I could well have been killed. After that the pressmen eased off and Jan and I were able to live in peace.

Looking back on that unhappy episode I was both hurt and

amazed by it all. I accept a footballer is news, but could not understand such interest in Jan and me. Wolves were hardly a glamour club such as Liverpool or Manchester United and my own career was going through one of its less successful periods. I was hurt as well because I like to think when it comes to the press, radio and television I've been one of the most accessible players over the years. Rarely do I say no to an interview or a picture and like to help the press as much as I can. We've got on well over the years and if anything I've been a soft touch when it's come to posing for pictures. They've had me in kilts running with a football at my feet, and at Everton I even dressed up in a tutu waving a magic wand with a pair of wellies on my feet for one stunt. People reckoned I looked like comedian Freddie Starr so they dressed me up like him. So, having always been friendly and cooperative, I was hurt the press chased me as they did over Amy. I know the sports reporter is a different breed from the newsmen and there are papers that enjoy digging up the dirt more than most, but Jan especially went through hell over our daughter and I think the whole episode was unfair and a gross invasion of our privacy.

It was harder for Jan than for me. I'd tussled with the glare of publicity many times before but to Jan it was totally alien. Tremendous pressure was put on us both but happily it's all behind us now as Jan and I have worked hard at getting our lives together to provide a home for Amy. Together with Jan, little Amy is the greatest thing that's ever happened to me. Life is worth living with her; one look at Amy makes the day a happy one. It's for her and Jan's sake that I plan to put down a few roots at last and make a permanent home in the Midlands. Her first few years have been like that of a gypsy. She's already had five homes and I don't think it's fair to keep moving so we've decided to settle in Birmingham. Most of our friends are there as well and with Jan being a local girl it makes sense to make the second city our home. Luckily we've a good set of friends, many of whom are outside the world of football. Although you make many acquaintances in soccer it's strange in a way how few become what I'd class as close friends. Having pals away from the game is a great help. I've kept in close touch with many of my old mates from Glasgow and although they're now married with families of their own we still see a lot of them. They've helped me be myself over the years and there's nothing I enjoy better than a quiet meal out with friends and not a word of football talk. Soccer is hard to get away from sometimes and I'm the sort of chap who takes his work home with him. If I've got worries at the club Jan will soon know and the worst for her comes on a Saturday if we've lost. Jan knows not to make any arrangements then as we'll often stay in and watch the telly. I'm not very good company when we've lost and it takes at least a couple of days to wipe away the depression. Sunday morning brings the papers and the match reports, so it's not until Monday that I switch back on again. Jan enjoys her football and fortunately her family have always been Aston Villa fans. Amy has been to see a few matches as well but she tends to get a little too excited and becomes a handful for Jan.

Away from soccer I suppose my biggest hobby is golf. My handicap are the clubs, but I'm hoping I might get a bit more time in the future to polish my swing. When I'm going well I can play off single figures and I've got what you would call a floating handicap, I suppose.

I still see an awful lot of my family. James comes across from Canada fairly frequently and never misses a big game, while Mum and Willie are always popping south of the border to see us. I'm closer to Duncan now, which is strange because as kids we were further apart. Duncs is now married with a little lad and also lives in Birmingham, so we get to see quite a lot of each other.

In so many respects I've come to terms with life now and sincerely hope the harrowing times are behind me. I told you I'd an eventful life off the field but from now on it's going to be roses all the way.

12 JUST FOR A LAUGH

Whoever it was that said football was a funny old game must be wishing now he owned the copyright on those few words. Never a week has gone by without a manager or a player trotting out that golden statement. However, it is true because through the years I've enjoyed some great moments of fun and laughter. Some of the great characters we've already met, and to set the laughs rolling who better to start with than the clown prince of soccer John "Budgie" Burridge. When he sits down to write his memoirs it will be more like a joke book as he recalls some of the craziest times you could think of.

When Budgie was transferred to the Wolves, as we were old mates, I invited him to stop with Jan and me until he found a house. One night Jan and I went out and left Budgie watching the television; when we came back we were a little alarmed to hear music pumping out of the windows and a shadowy figure jumping around in the lounge. We crept in and peeped through the door to see Budgie in full flight. I'm not sure whether he was Mick Jagger or Rod Stewart but Budgie had stripped to the waist and, using a snooker cue as a pretend microphone, was miming to the record. I swear to this day that when he looked up and discovered us watching it was the only time I ever saw him blush.

While he was stopping with us Budgie devised a new training schedule in our lounge. He was a fitness fanatic and on a Friday night he'd appear to watch the telly with his goalkeeping gloves on Budgie would lie on the settee and my job was to test his reflexes. With the fruit bowl in front of me I would lob apples and oranges at him without warning and Budgie had to catch

149

them. What we must have looked like heaven knows, as Budgie threw himself around the room as if he was at Wembley on Cup Final Day.

Another classic story is when Budgie was serving his soccer apprenticeship at Workington Town. The manager took him aside one day in training to brush up on one or two finer points. "Now son," he said. "You're going to find yourself sometimes in a one-to-one situation when a striker comes bursting through and he's only got you to beat. What I want you to practise is running out of your goal as fast as you can and throwing yourself at his feet. But more important is when you throw yourself at him shout in a loud voice, 'Geronimo!' I've always found it puts them off and they're so surprised you get the ball or they just miss." Budgie took note of this and sure enough after a handful of matches in goal for Workington the situation arose. Much to the manager's horror the striker walked around Budgie as if he wasn't there and calmly planted the ball in the back of the net. At half-time the manager was waiting for an explanation from Budgie. "Jesus Christ, son didn't you remember what I told you about shouting at them," he cried. "I did everything you told me to boss until I got there and I couldn't remember the frigging Indian's name."

Two last stories of Budgie come from continental trips. At the end of one season tour we were sunbathing around a pool in Magalluf when a German tourist started to show off by performing a series of high dives. Everytime he dived we got soaked as the water splashed out of the pool onto us. Eventually Budgie got fed up. He sprang up and then proceeded to walk around the pool on his hands. He even climbed up the ladder on his hands and then performed an immaculate dive with flips and somersaults and entered the water with hardly a ripple. He climbed out and strode past the German, who by now had got the message and was hiding underneath his sun umberella. On another trip back from a European match Budgie played a wicked prank on Villa manager Ron Saunders and to this day he swears it was one of the reasons which led to his transfer from Villa Park. Saunders was a terrible flier. He couldn't face a journey without a brandy or two in his stomach and as we came in to land at Birmingham one night Budgie prepared his trick. He blew up the sick bag and just as we were about to touch down he exploded it behind the manager's seat. The Villa boss went white with fear and his assistant Roy McLaren jumped up to tear a strip off Budgie. "The man could have had a heart attack, you idiot," he said. Budgie just grinned, but Mr Saunders was not amused.

Another time we ran in to trouble on a foreign trip was when Wolves were in Sweden one time. Along with Ken Hibbitt, Billy Kellock and defender Alan Dodd, I'd been out for a walk around and a couple of beers. When we got back to the hotel someone suggested a bite to eat so we all trouped off to the local branch of Macdonalds. We ordered a hamburger each and then mad Billy Kellock and Alan Dodd started arguing about how much they could eat and who was the hungriest. In the end they challenged each other to an eating contest so, to the bewilderment of the restaurant, we ordered up as many hamburgers as they could make. Ken and I acted as judges as Billy and Alan went to their task like two hamsters. Their cheeks were bulging as they ate their way through the buns. In the end Billy Kellock was declared the winner by four Big Macs and one regular to Alan Dodd's four Big Macs. It was the most expensive meal that I'd had in a long time as we didn't get back to the team hotel until 12.30 and midnight was the deadline. In the morning we were fined £25 each for stopping out too late, and seeing we had a match coming up thought it best not to tell Wolves manager Graham Hawkins where we'd been or what we'd been up to.

Poor old Wolves have had to put up with a lot in recent years and towards the end of my time there they were the target for every joke or wisecrack from the terraces. Like the chap who walks into a pub in Wolverhampton and sits next to a dog on a stool by the bar. The dog is watching Match of the Day on the telly between Manchester United and Wolves and when United score the dog jumps up does a couple of somersaults and downs a pint of bitter. "That's fantastic," says the chap "Tell me landlord what does he do when Wolves score?" "Don't know," says the landlord, "I've only had him six months!" Another favourite was when a big match was coming up against either Liverpool or Spurs, Graham Hawkins used to take us to the local job centre for training – so we could get used to big crowds! Or the three managers in a pub story: Ron Atkinson of United, Everton's Howard Kendall and Graham Hawkins are having a drink when a fourth ghostly figure appears at their table with a pint in his hand. The mystery man turns out to be God who grants the managers one question each. "Tell me," says Ron Atkinson, "When will United do the League and Cup double?" "Not for forty-two years" says God. "You'll win the League and the Cup before then but you'll have to wait for the double." Atkinson thinks for a moment and shrugs his shoulders. "I won't be around then," he says. Kendall is next: "Tell me God, when will we win the League again." "Not for twenty-six years," says God. "So I won't be around then," replies Kendall. Last, it's Hawkins' chance: "Tell me when will Wolves with the Cup?" God draws breath . . . "I don't think I'll be around then!"

The Wolverhampton folk or the Black Country people have very dry sense of humour which is best illustrated by a wonderful story of when Villa chief scout Don Dorman went to sign a promising young lad. Don had been watching this strapping young lad for some time and when he called at the family's home found they were all big and built like mountains. There were three boys all over six foot tall and about as wide, while dad was even bigger and mum too was a well-built, handsome lady. So Don politely asks the father what the secret of having such a strong healthy family is. "Stew," says the dad. "Mother's speciality is home made stew. It's grand stuff and will make a man of any- one." They then went off to the local pub to have a drink and chat about the lad signing as a professional footballer. Don is invited back to the house eventually, for a plate of mum's legendary stew as the pot is always on the boil. And sure enough the stew is the best he's ever tasted. On the way out Don happens to see the family's pet bull mastiff dog lying in front of the fire and can't ignore the fact that the animal is better endowed than any other he's ever seen. He asks the dad about it and jokes whether the dog eats the stew as well. Dad answers in his thick Black Country accent: "No, it's amazing really, he only licks the plates!"

On Merseyside, too, I had some laughs and John Bailey, the Everton full-back, was usually at the centre of the fun. John had a habit of getting his words mixed or muddled up and just before the Cup Final had the dressing room baffled when he proudly announced he'd spent his bonus on a new Winchester. He went on for some time about how he'd always wanted a Winchester and had been saving up for ages to have one specially made. We were all a little mystified since none of us knew John was keen on shooting and sure enough he'd got his words mixed up. It wasn't a Winchester he'd bought but a Chesterfield settee. Another great character at Goodison was coach Terry Darracott who was always full of fun. The best story about him was when he and some of the other lads went to Glasgow for the presentation of the Manager of the Year award to Howard Kendall. They went out on the town that night to celebrate and Terry, who didn't know Glasgow, was determined to enjoy himself but was worried about drinking too much and getting lost. So before he went out he walked into reception and calmly asked the girl behind the desk if she had a felt tip pen. To her amazement Terry stuck his bald head over the counter and asked her to write the name of the hotel, The Albany, in felt tip on his head. This she did and off Terry went to enjoy himself on the town. In the early hours he stumbled into a taxi and of course by now had completely forgotten where he was staying. "Where to mister?" asked the cab driver. Terry looked blank and then just leant forward and pointed towards his head and the words "The Albany Hotel".

I'm sure people must look at footballers and think us a strange, if not daft lot, but there are times when we can have a joke at the expense of some of the reporters or commentators who follow us around. Over the years I've collected some great gaffs like the time Dickie Davies was hosting a programme and at half-time asked one of the experts, Denis Law "What's the manager going to be telling his team at half-time Denis?" Back came Denis with the immortal line "He'll be telling them there's forty-five minutes left!" David Coleman has set the standard through the years for making slip-ups like "Nottingham Forest are having a bad run. They've lost six matches without a win." Or how about, "With the very last kick of the game Bobby McDonald scored with a header." One of my favourites is from Brian Moore of ITV when he was commentating on a cup final and said, "And now the familiar sight of Liverpool lifting the League Cup for the first time."

People always poke fun at Scottish football and the all-time classic came from Gary Newbon on Midlands TV one Sunday afternoon when he said, "There'll be more football in a moment but first we've got the highlights of the Scottish League Cup Final." Then there was David Coleman again reading out the teleprinter results "Ayr United 1 Arbroath 0; Arbroath still without an away win of any kind." Or how about Frank Bough on Grandstand a few years ago when he said, "Kilmarnock versus Partick Thistle, match postponed. That is, of course, a latest score." And two more classics, one from Sheffield Wednesday boss Howard Wilkinson, who was quoted once as saying, "I'm a firm believer that if you score one goal, the other team has to score two to win."

You can't match the Merseyside humour though and two of the best examples I've experienced came in letters from fans. When I left Goodison one Evertonian wrote to Villa Park and said:

"Please would you be kind enough to pass on this letter of thanks to your new boy Andy Gray. If he does for you what he did for us in two years Everton might have some competition at the top.

Actually, if I found Andy in bed with my missus, I'd tuck him up to make sure he didn't catch a cold – that's how highly I rate him.

Yours in sport,
PEDRO BISHOP."

Thanks for the laugh, and my compliments to Mrs Bishop.

Another priceless piece of Merseyside humour came by of another letter, this time from a rather strange set of solicitors.

TAKIM TUDOR KLEENIS AND WYNNE
PRACTISING SOLICITORS
(hoping to get it right soon)

Mr A. Fearns E.F.C.F.O.R.C.U.P.
Kirby
Merseyside

Mr Andy Gray,
c/o Everton Football Club
Goodison Park,
Liverpool.

Dear Mr Gray,
We write on behalf of our client Mr Austin Fearns. Because of
your brilliant actions during the European Cup Winners semi-
final 2nd leg match on Wednesday, 23rd April 1985, when you
scored an important goal, our client received an injury to his
right knee by jumping into the air in the confined space of the
Lower Bullens Road stand. At 49 years of age and 17 stone, this
action proved to be very dangerous.

Since the match, our client has limped to the Norwich game
and incurred the added expense of buying a stand ticket instead
of taking his usual place in the Gladwys Street enclosure, feeling
that should you score again he would only incur minor scalding
from his luke warm coffee.

We feel that enough pressure is on your shoulders, so instead
of the usual court case where Mr Fearns would win substantial
compensation he has agreed to settle for a cup final ticket and
will pay any expenses which may be incurred by yourself.
He looks forward to hearing from you.

Yours sincerely
A.F. FEARNS
EVERTON SUPPORTER

And if I still needed convincing that Mr Fearns was worthy of a
cup final ticket, how about this for a burst of verse.

ODE TO ANDY GRAY

I really don't intend to sue,
That letter's just a ploy,
I've got to get to Wembley,
But up to now . . . no joy!!

How could I sue our Andy Gray!
A man who'd die for us,
Who'd head whatever's centred,
Even a Crosville bus!!

He's number one in all the world,
I swear . . . there's no-one better,
His courage has instilled in me,
The guts to write this letter.

So Andy . . . help me get there,
To bring the trophy back,
I promise I'll relinquish,
My title . . . sassenach!!

I'll roar when you lead Scotland,
You'll hear me shout, Go! Go!
To help take Jock Stein's army,
Across to Mexico!!

But if I can't to Wembley go,
There's just one thing to say,
Go out and "do it" Andy,
I'm with you all the way!!!!

Sadly there were no tickets spare not even for the bard of Goodison, but to show my thanks how about the reply conjured up with the help of my cousin.

ODE TO A.F. FEARNS – EVERTON SUPPORTER

To the Rabbie Burns o' Kirkby,
From the front of the Blues,
Thanks for your good wishes,
I hope that we don't lose,

'Cos since I've moved to Goodison,
I know how much it means,
To all good Evertonians,
To see fulfilled their dreams,

It's Wembley after Rotterdam,
The fans will come with pride,
I've been asked for tickets,
From places far and wide,

My brother's here from Canada,
With half a dozen mates,
My mother's down from Scotland,
I've got cousins at the gates,

The players do get tickets,
But we only get so many,
And all my ration has been used,
So now I haven't any,

So while I'd like to help you,
There's not much I can do,
But I sincerely hope you make it,
'Cos you sound a real TRUE BLUE.

As I was saying, football's a funny old game!

13 GOODISON GLORY DAYS

November 1983 brought more fireworks than I can ever remember as my career turned upside down again. On bonfire night it was Wolves who were going up in smoke as we crashed to a 5-0 defeat at Nottingham Forest. The Wanderers were bottom of the division and needed a couple of sticks of dynamite to shift them.

Within days though, I was on the move to Everton and little did I realise then but that week the blue fuse paper was lit on the most exciting eighteen months of my career. I wish it could have been longer but with an FA Cup medal, a League Championship win and victory in the European Cup Winners Cup it was a time when everyone's dreams came true. It was like a party really with an endless supply of fun. And yet the strange thing is that Andy Gray so nearly missed it all, or rather nearly turned his back on it. On Everton's road to Wembley I was dropped for the first time in my career and was set to walk out on Goodison. Fortunately my head won over my hurt pride and for once in my life I kept my big mouth shut.

The chance to play for Everton came literally out of the blue. I think I knew, as you often do sometimes, that my career with Wolves was nearing an end. My contract was due to expire at the end of the 1983-84 season and although I was fond of Wolves there was no way I was going to drop down into the second division. The move to Goodison started rolling three days after Wolves had been roasted at Forest. After training on Tuesday Ken Hibbitt and I, with a couple of other lads, went for lunch in a pub just five minutes away from Molineux. The meal turned into an inquest on what was going wrong at

Wolves. Both Ken and I were desperately concerned with the team's performance and realised that unless something was done soon the club would be struggling like never before. We chatted for hours and it must have been near five o'clock by the time I got home. Jan was waiting for me with an urgent message to phone the Wolves manager Graham Hawkins at his office at Molineux. "What's he want, do you think?" she asked. "I think I've got an idea," I said as I reached for the phone. The Wolves manager must have been waiting for my call as the phone hardly rang before he answered. He wouldn't tell me anything over the phone other than he needed to see me in his office as soon as possible to discuss some business that had come up. Now to a footballer that really means only one thing – a transfer.

I'd told Jan only a couple of weeks before I felt we'd be on the move before long and sure enough the call had come, but as I set off for Molineux I didn't have a clue where the next stop was going to be. Several clubs had been linked with me in the papers but that really didn't mean a thing. Graham Hawkins soon put me out of my misery – Everton had agreed to pay £200,000 for me. The clubs had already agreed terms and Howard Kendall, the Goodison manager, wanted to see me in the morning. The decision to sell me had been a board one at Molineux. With my contract running out at the end of the season the directors were keen to get money for me while they could and without appearing big-headed I was one of the best assets or most sellable player they had. Graham Hawkins, who I got on well with, was not in favour of the move. He knew the money would go straight into the bank to pay off debts, and for him it must have been like another nail in the coffin. Mind you Everton were hardly having a rosy time. They were only five places off the bottom of the first division themselves and manager Howard Kendall was weathering a battle to keep his job. To make things even worse they'd just lost 3-0 to Liverpool in the derby game at Anfield so, for me, it was like jumping out of the frying pan into the fire.

I travelled to Liverpool on the Wednesday morning and arrived at the ground too early so nipped into a nearby newsagents to buy a paper. The chap behind the counter knowing his soccer obviously recognised me and as soon as I left was on the phone to the local paper to tip them off that Andy Gray was visiting Goodison. So by the time I got to meet Howard Kendall the secret was out. The papers had been on the phone which can't have pleased the Everton boss that much. I found him a straight and sound individual who appeared to be coping with the pressure pretty well. He'd watched me play for Wolves in a Milk Cup tie at Preston earlier in the season. That surprised me even more. It was one of my worst matches and I joked with Howard Kendall that he must be desperate and was he still sure he wanted to sign me. His big problem was that Graeme Sharp, his regular number nine, had been injured against Liverpool and on his own admission he was keen to sign a striker. We more or less agreed on a deal that day, but on the Thursday met again. This time I had my accountant Tony Price with me to sort out a contract.Tony has been my accountant for several years and is also a very good friend. He's helped me no end with financial advice and has mastermined all the paper work behind my moves to Wolves, Everton and then back to Villa. As a player I'm not very keen on agents but these days the financial dealings surrounding footballers can become so complicated that anyone who tries to sort things out by themself would be a fool. I know I can rely on Tony to go through all the small print and it's crucial to have a good man like him. Footballers can earn a lot over a short period and it's vital to have some expert guidance about pensions and so on and it makes life so much easier when you've got a good pal like Tony to rely on.

There were still problems over a contract and in the end I signed a temporary one so Everton could get me registered in time to play against Forest on Saturday. Then the only other hurdle was the medical and for me this was the most nerve-wracking moment of all. Along with club physiotherapist, John Clinkard, I went down to a local hospital for the usual X-rays and check-up. The medical was very thorough, perhaps the toughest I've had, and once again a specialist and the club doctor spent ages poking and prodding my suspect knee which had just had another kick on it and looked sore. When they were finished John and I were ordered out into the waiting room where we sat for what seemed like hours. Finally we were called in again and both the doctor and the specialist looked unsure. "Tell us Andy, how do you feel about your knee?" asked the doc. "It's taken some stick, but I think it's fine. I can play on it as well as ever," I replied. "And what if Everton didn't sign you what would you be doing on Saturday?" was his next question. "Playing for Wolves, of course, I'm fighting fit." That seemed to satisfy both the doctor and the specialist who nodded at each other and announced they were happy with my medical.

So, it was Goodison Park for me and strangely enough for the first time in my life I was nervous about moving. Daft really, because here I was an experienced player with my twenty-eighth birthday just a few weeks away, a tried and trusted international, who was worried about a transfer. I suppose when I moved to Aston Villa I was still too young to appreciate the importance of it. When I left for Wolves and that staggering fee I was cocksure of myself but over the last few months with Wolves my confidence had taken a bit of a battering. For the first time in my career I felt I was on trial and had to work harder than ever to prove myself. Joining a club such as Everton was also a daunting prospect. Everyone was quick to remind me of the centre forwards who had graced Goodison over the years. There'd been the legendary sixty goals a season Dixie Dean, then that England hero Tommy Lawton. In more recent times the Everton fans had idolised Alex Young, the man they called the Golden Vision. He was followed by the likes of big Joe Royle and then Bob Latchford, so as you can see the Goodison folk had come to expect a lot from their centre forwards.

Fortunately I settled well at Everton, one big reason being that arriving on Merseyside was like going home to Glasgow. When you compare the two they have an awful lot in common: geographically they are both big industrial cities served by rivers, Liverpool by the Mersey and Glasgow by the Clyde; the industries are similar and in past years they've both suffered hard at the hands of unemployment; they both have two major football teams; and probably the most important thing of all the humour is irresistable. When you consider the plight of the average worker in either Glasgow or Liverpool they must have less to laugh about than anyone; an increasing majority spend their lives searching for work and struggling to survive and yet their laughter is as rich and as genuine as anyone's. In Liverpool, as in Glasgow, I think you're born with a sense of humour and you certainly need one to survive. So, for me, Merseyside became a second home and that first week with Everton turned out to be a significant one for everyone at the club. Colin Harvey, an old playing partner of the manager's, who along with Alan Ball had formed arguably one the finest midfields ever seen in English football was promoted to first team coach; Peter Reid made a comeback in midfield after injury; and goalkeeper Neville Southall found his form.

On my first Saturday with Everton we beat Nottingham Forest 1-0. Then after losing to Arsenal and Norwich scored a much needed morale boosting 1-0 win over Manchester United at Old Trafford. Then came Aston Villa and my first goal for Everton in a 1-1 draw, but after that we struggled again. We lost at Queens Park Rangers, drew with Sunderland and then slumped to a most humiliating 3-0 defeat to Wolves at Molineux, two days after Christmas.

There wasn't much spirit of goodwill in the Everton dressing room that day I can tell you. For me it was a massive blow and for the team in general, and especially the manager, the pressure was beginning to build. The "Kendall Out" campaign was stronger than ever, and if not for the admirable support of **Everton chairman Philip Carter the club would have been looking for a new manager. Many clubs would have sacked** Howard Kendall there and then, but Mr Carter's resistance to bow to public pressure paid off and it must go down as one of the wisest decisions ever made by a football chairman. The crunch really came at New Year. We were due to play Birmingham City at St. Andrews and before the game Howard Kendall gave us a long hard team talk. He accused some players of not pulling their weight and threatened wholesale changes unless we started getting results. That did the trick and suddenly every player became passionately aware of his responsibility. We beat Birmingham 2-0 and never looked back again.

Everton only lost three more League games and within weeks were on the road to Wembley in both the Milk Cup and the FA

Cup. Our run in the FA Cup started with a 2-0 win at Stoke in the third round but it so nearly finished for everyone, and for me especially, in the fourth round when we faced third division Gillingham. In the first game at Goodison we scrambled a goalless draw. I missed a good chance and Gillingham gave us the fright of our lives by hitting the bar. The replay was the following Tuesday and we travelled down to Kent fully expecting a hard time. We were having our usual pre-match meal when Howard Kendall beckoned me outside for a quiet word. I was **still chewing on my last mouthful of steak as he gave me one of the worst shocks I've ever had: "I've decided not to play you against Gillingham tonight Andy. I've had to pick the team which I think can do the job, and I'm afraid it doesn't include you."** To say I was devastated is an understatement. I was totally amazed at his decision. I'd been playing as well as any of the others and my surprise or shock at being left out soon turned to anger. I was just about to tell Howard Kendall to shove it and walk out of the team's headquarters when I managed for once to control my emotions. I swallowed hard and told him I didn't **agree with his decision which I thought was totally unjustified. He'd made his mind up though, and there was obviously no point in me arguing with him. Howard Kendall turned to go back into the dining room and I paused. Shall I go back in or shall I just clear out now? That was the decision. I only had a couple of seconds to decide and thankfully someone up there guided me through the doors to rejoin the Everton team. Heaven** knows what would have happened if I'd staged my one man walk-out. Had it been a League match I think I might have gone ahead and walked off but because it was such a vital cup game I knew deep down I could not let the rest of the team and supporters down.

I did get to play, albeit as substitute, against Gillingham that night when once again the third division team gave us a hard time. We drew 0-0 again thanks to a brilliant save from Neville Southall, but eventually won the replay 3-0, and after that I was never dropped again. I had a hand in all three goals in the replay and that convinced Howard Kendall of my worth. After that victory the Everton manager and I shared some drinks on the team coach and he was big enough to admit that leaving me out had been a mistake. I respected straight talk like that and although I'd been hurt by him, he was always very fair after that. He had a hard job as well because Everton were on the way to Wembley in the Milk Cup. I couldn't play in the matches having been cup tied with Wolves so every time there was a Milk Cup game he chopped and changed the side. And even though they kept winning I was always recalled immediately for an FA Cup tie or a League match although there were times when I wondered whether I'd make it. After beating Aston Villa in the semi-final and reaching Wembley I honestly thought Howard Kendall would have to stick by the same team for the next match, but he brought me back. Watching Everton play Liverpool in the first ever all Merseyside Cup Final was frustrating. We deserved to win and even though you belong to a club it's never the same watching from the touchline. When Liverpool won the replay 1-0 our determination to make amends in the FA Cup was stronger than ever.

In the League we had pulled ourselves up to half-way and like a battleship preparing for a major confrontation all decks at Goodison were cleared with Wembley on the horizon again. We dispensed with Shrewsbury and Notts County and the last hurdle was Southampton in the semi-final at Highbury. It was a cracker of a game with Adrian Heath, "Inchy" as we called him, hitting the only goal in extra time. The match was best summed up by the Saints boss, Laurie McMenemy, who's never at a loss for words. Afterwards he said "I looked round my dressing room before the game and there were experienced players nervous and anxious. I watched Everton run out and there wasn't a nerve amongst them, so I feared the worst." And that summed us up. We had so much confidence and belief in ourselves that we were convinced no side could beat us. Even if we went a goal behind, we knew we'd win. And that's why we won the FA Cup. Every single player was convinced we were going to win. I know before a big match all players say they're confident and every team goes out to win, but before the final against Watford I've never been with such a confident team.

We didn't travel to London until the day before the final

which was our usual routine. None of the players liked being away from home couped up in a hotel, so come the day of the match we all felt relaxed and rearing to go. My brother James came across from Canada to join all the family at Wembley and it certainly turned out to be a day to remember. Once we'd found our feet and weathered Watford's early storm we were never in danger of losing. Graeme Sharp got the first and I got the second, which really clinched the cup and what a great feeling it was to be a winner again. As we went on a lap of honour and celebrated our cup win I felt I'd won my own private battle to prove I was still a top player. That season was really make or break for me. If I'd stayed with Wolves my career would have gone on the decline, but here I was at Wembley with the FA Cup in one hand and my winner's medal in the other. No footballer could ever want for more. It was a make or break season for Everton as well. The cup run had lifted them to their most successful time for years and more important, we felt the Merseyside crown coming our way.

When I first arrived at Everton one of the first things that hit me was how the Goodison club and its supporters lived in the shadow of Liverpool. You often saw Evertonians casting envious glances across Stanley Park to Anfield as Liverpool raced away with the honours. Goodison football folk had been made to feel like second class citizens for years but that season Everton began to hit back. And the match that did it was the return derby game at Goodison. Liverpool had swept into the lead with an Ian Rush goal but in the second half Everton emerged from their self-imposed soccer exile to grab a draw. Walking off that day we all felt we had finally laid the Liverpool jinx and from then on we had as much right as them to rule Merseyside. Everton finally proved their point at the start of the 1984-85 season with a win over Liverpool in the Charity Shield. Sadly it was a game I missed out on. I'd been injured in the run-up to the match and although I was fully fit couldn't win a place in the team. I was overjoyed for Everton but depressed at not being a part of it and at the end I hadn't the heart to go on the lap of honour with the rest of the team.

The start of Everton's championship season was for me a

long, hard and at times lonely struggle. For the League kick-off against Spurs at Goodison Howard Kendall relied on the team that had won the Charity Shield, which meant I was on the bench as substitute again. It was a disastrous start for us all. We lost 4-1 and after coming on as substitute towards the end I limped off injured. That was me out again for another couple of weeks but I came back after scoring a couple of goals in the reserves, although my recall nearly blew into a major dressing room row.

I was given the number nine shirt against Newcastle United at St James Park but my joy at being back was tempered by the disappointment I felt for my old mate Graeme Sharp whose place I'd been given. Sharpy was distraught at being dropped as the team was just begining to settle down and things were moving very sweetly. Before the game I was with Graeme and just as we were about to get changed he pulled me to one side to ask some advice. He was clearly upset and was fingering a letter in his jacket pocket. "I've written out a transfer request Andy and I'm going to hand it to the boss after the game," he said. "I don't want to leave but I'm not going to be dropped like this again." Imagine how I felt. I was the bloke who'd taken his place and here he was turning to me for advice. "Don't be daft. You can't ask for a transfer, it's only this game you've been left out for, there's bound to be another chance," I argued. Sharpy was not sure what to do but before the match I made him promise he wouldn't hand the letter in until we'd had a chance to sit down and talk it over. "Never act on impulse," I told him which from my own track record was a fine piece of advice from me. And as it turned out Sharpy was back in the next week at my expense. I got a goal against Newcastle but also cracked a bone in my foot and that meant a few more weeks on the injury list. I was out of action for six weeks and during that time Everton emerged as championship challengers.

When I was finally fit again I was back in the squad but only as substitute. I made the number twelve shirt my own during what must surely be one of the most frustrating periods of my entire career. I was sub for about six or seven weeks and sat and watched as Everton went to the top of the table. We were playing some super football and I was professional enough to realise that Howard Kendall could not change a winning side. The run started on October 13th. We beat Villa 2-1 and then at Anfield overcame Liverpool in the derby game. Sharpy scored the only goal and that famous win was worth double the points in prestige and pride. We rolled on to crush Manchester United 5-0, and then swept aside Leicester, West Ham and Stoke to lead the first division by three points. In between my stints as substitute I was playing in the reserves to keep up my match fitness and was getting more and more depressed. I couldn't see a way back into the first team and, with all due respect, Everton reserve football was not really my cup of tea. I was playing well when I had the chance, but I feared the longer I was out the more my form and confidence would suffer. There were even whispers of a transfer. Aston Villa for one were interested, and that sort of news was very unsettling. Although I was unhappy I was still proud to be part of the Everton set-up and hadn't thought about the prospect of moving on again. Most days after training I'd return home in a miserable mood and the only chap who really kept me going was reserve coach Terry Darracott. He was always full of laughter and humour and he went out of his way to keep me happy.

Football is such a strange game at times and holds so many surprises and just when I was resigning myself to a move my Goodison career opened up again. Unfortunately the chance came when Adrian Heath tore all the ligaments in his knee in the match against Sheffield Wednesday. I was desperately sorry for Adrian and felt guilty at first that I was cashing in on his misfortune. His injury opened the door to a regular first team place and I found myself back in the attack for the main championship clashes. There was just a point in it between ourselves and Manchester United and Arsenal. Spurs, Southampton and a group of other clubs weren't far behind either. We lost the lead before Christmas after losing at home to Chelsea but slipped back into gear again in the New Year. Sharp and Sheedy were getting the goals and although I was playing well my confidence was beginning to suffer. For the life of me I couldn't get a goal and for a striker there's nothing worse than not scoring. Playing well is little consolation because my job and enjoyment in football has always come from hitting the back of the net.

My problems were highlighted when Everton played non-Leaguers Telford United in the fifth round of the FA Cup. I did everything but score. One header shaved the bar, a shot squeezed past the post, but the ball just wouldn't bounce my way. I could feel the crowd at Goodison willing me on. They were as desperate and as keen as I was to see me score a goal and I began to wonder if I'd lost the touch. Fortunately everything came right a week later in a match at Leicester. Two strange things happened at Filbert Street to prove why some footballers are often superstitious. The match was being televised and before the game one of the television boys came into the dressing room to check a few facts and figures. "Do you realise Andy that you've scored ninety-eight League goals in this country?" he said. "Another two today would bring the century, that would be nice on the box," he added. I laughed and joked I'd be happy with just one the way my luck had been running, but he set me thinking. Players rarely keep a check on how many games they've played in or goals they've scored and the facts and figures usually mean more to the press lads. But as I sat and waited in the dressing room I suddenly thought about reaching that hundred mark.

At Leicester there was a reshuffle because Graeme Sharp was injured and that meant his place was being taken by Alan Harper. Now Sharpy always wore the number nine shirt which meant I'd had to play in eight. Ever since I started my soccer I'd been a number nine and enjoyed wearing the centre forward or striker's shirt. Because Graeme was injured I took the chance to wear his number nine and it worked a treat. We beat Leicester 2-1 and after four months without a goal I cracked in both of them to reach the century mark. Television made a meal of it and I felt immensely happy and relieved at having finally made some major contribution to Everton's title bid. After that I kept hold of the number nine shirt and it certainly brought me a lucky run.

Everton cruised through to take the title with an amazing

burst of form. Starting on Boxing Day and finishing in May with a win over Queens Park Rangers which clinched the championship, we played seventeen matches and of these won fifteen and drew two. Nobody could live with us and for me and most of the other Everton lads the title was really clinched in London the night we beat Spurs at White Hart Lane. It was billed as the championship decider. There were only three points between us at the time and in front of just over 48,000 fans we overpowered the Spurs to win 2-1. That night we felt the title was ours and suddenly a chance of taking the treble was alive.

We were through to the semi-finals of both the European Cup Winners Cup and the FA Cup, and faced both in the same week. First we travelled to Germany to tackle Bayern Munich and a 0-0 draw in the first leg was, for us, an important result. On the Saturday it was off to Villa Park to face Luton in the semi-final of the FA Cup and we squeezed through that one by the skin of our teeth. The European match had been hard and I think most of us had been drained both physically and mentally. Luton killed us in the first half and thoroughly deserved their half-time lead. In the break we managed to take stock and it was our experience and cunning that finally took us through to Wembley.

People talked a lot about pressure in the hectic spell towards the end of the season but to be honest none of us had time to get worried. We were like robots towards the end as we moved from match to match. The opposition all looked the same and it was a question of going out day after day and switching on. Once the League title was under our belt we could concentrate on the two cups but I don't know what it is about the English League but nothing is made easy for you. The League season had been a demanding one and now we were being asked to face two finals in four days. On Wednesday it was all off to Rotterdam for the Cup Winners Cup final against Rapid Vienna and then back to Wembley to face Manchester United in the traditional end of season showpiece. In a way the two games were so close we didn't really have time to enjoy either. The night in Rotterdam was a magical one as Everton powered to a 3-1 win and their first European win.

History had been made, and all of us were delighted and thrilled at our achievement. But we all knew we couldn't afford to celebrate too hard and within hours of winning the Cup Winners Cup we were on the way back home to prepare for Wembley. We didn't even have time to unpack our cases; an afternoon at home and then it was back on the coach for the journey south. The triumph in Europe hadn't given us any time to worry or grow nervous about the FA Cup Final and most of us thought we could float through Manchester United on a high. We knew, of course, it was perhaps going to be the toughest match yet but things had been rolling along so well we could not see ourselves being beaten. The treble awaited and on Cup Final day we felt as relaxed and as confident as we had done the year before.

Within minutes of kicking off though I think we all realised how much the European match had taken out of us. We lost to United because we were missing that extra spark. Along with all the other lads I felt tired after only ten minutes and when your legs feel heavy at half-time you know it's not a good sign. We certainly had the will to win because more than anything we wanted that League and Cup double, but our bodies wouldn't respond. When United went down to ten men, we could and should have overpowered them, but the long season had finally caught up with us on the Wembley pitch. Manchester United, to give them credit, fought hard for the cup but I'm convinced we could have won the treble given a little more time in between finals. Another couple of days rest would have made so much difference and with it we could have beaten Manchester United.

Losing the treble was a blow and missing out at Wembley was even worse. A win there would have rounded off a fabulous season in style but I can hardly compain. I enjoyed more success in that glorious Goodison year than most players have in a lifetime.

14 MATCHES AND MEN TO REMEMBER

Everton's championship year will go down in bold print in the record books and for us all at Goodison we felt we had written our names into history. The 1984-85 season was by far the best in my career as far as winning goes. The League Championship and the European Cup Winners Cup were more than I hoped for and at the end of the season I'd achieved what many players can only dream of.

Over the years I'd won every English cup, the championship, the FA and the League or Milk Cup, as it is now known, and on top of that a major European trophy. I'd played for Scotland as well and been voted the players' Player of the Year. Not a bad haul. People have always asked me about the matches and men I remember best. There are six games that really stand out in my mind for various reasons: some are landmarks and others I remember purely because they were wonderful contests.

The first match in my collection would be Everton's Cup Winners Cup semi-final against the German side Bayern Munich. We drew the first leg over there 0-0 and so home advantage favoured us in the return. A win was vital, of course, because Everton were desperate to show they too, like Liverpool, could become a major force in European football.

A crowd of just under 50,000 filled Goodison for the second leg and witnessed one of the finest games of football ever played on the ground. Bayern took the lead in the first half through Hoeness, and at the break we went in trailing by that one goal. With away goals counting double in the event of a draw in European matches our task was even greater but Howard Kendall was still confident in the dressing room: "You're doing

173

all right lads. Don't worry. If we keep on going we're bound to get a goal and I'm sure the fans will suck one in as well for us." And sure enough the fans rose to the challenge as did the Everton side. Recently football crowds have come in for a lot of hammer because of hooliganism, but the night of the Bayern Munich match the Everton fans were truly superb. They lifted the team to victory and so strong was their support none of the players felt they could let them down by losing. The Germans did not have a chance when you think about it. You see they weren't just playing against eleven men; that night there were at least 45,000 working for victory. Graeme Sharp got the equaliser from a long throw and when the ball hit the back of the net Goodison erupted. I don't think I've ever been overcome by so much noise and you could see that Bayern were suffering. The fight went out of them as we charged forward in wave upon wave of attacks. With twenty minutes to go I gave Everton the lead. It was a scrappy goal which just crept in and the boss had been right . . . the crowd sucked it over the line. Once again the ground celebrated in a volcano of noise as the singing and shouting thundered around Goodison. By now we knew the Germans had no stomach for a battle and when Trevor Steven hit the third, we were on the way to the final. At the whistle I went to shake the hand of Hoeness who, to my surprise, turned angrily and shouted, "That was not football . . . you crazy men." It had been a hard game all right, but Everton had won fair and square and I think his outburst was just a severe case of sour grapes.

Another memorable match for me was Everton's FA Cup semi-final with Southampton at Highbury the season before. I've always found that semi-finals are more tense and difficult than finals and more often than not you get a better game. I suppose with a semi-final victory is so desperately important. No one ever remembers a losing semi-finalist whereas if you lose a cup final it's still an honour to be there.

The Southampton game was another tense and tight match. There was little to choose between the sides but on the day Everton were calmer and more confident, and we certainly needed to be as the game went into extra time. It was a match full of cut and thrust football as both teams took it in turns to attack. In extra time the tension was unbearable as we knew one goal was all that was needed to reach Wembley. And when Adrian Heath scored the feeling of achievement and relief was hard to describe. I'd never played in an FA Cup Final before and nor had the others. Wembley and Cup Final day has its own romantic magic, but when that whistle went against Southampton it was one of the most satisfying results of my career. I remember that game for the journey home as well. As we travelled back up the M1 and M6 motorways the road was full of Evertonians. Their colours were flying from car and coach windows and when they saw the team coach they hooted and waved in delight. I wished that journey could have lasted longer; it was great to see so many happy people. Merseyside doesn't have a lot to smile about in everyday life but here were thousands of people celebrating like never before.

Another semi-final which I include in my collection was one in the League Cup between Aston Villa and Queens Park Rangers. It was in the 1976-77 season, the year ironically that Villa beat Everton at the third attempt in the final. The three final games were quite something, but for me the Queens Park Rangers match was the best of the lot. In the first leg we drew 0-0 at Loftus Road and the second leg at Villa Park was the match I really enjoyed. It went into extra time before finishing all square at two apiece. Again it was a cliffhanger of a match, with nearly 48,500 fans packed into the ground. One funny thing about my memorable matches is that I failed to score in most; against QPR it was John Deehan who got both goals. There was a penalty save and plenty of drama as both sides fought it out in a breathtaking duel. Everything good in football was in that match. The ball cracked against the post and bar on countless occasions, both keepers saved their sides with some brilliant stops and every player gave his all. If anyone wanted an advert for British football I think I'd sit them down and let them watch a film of that game. Even words like epic and sensational hardly do it justice – it was a game I could play over and over again. And for Villa there was a happy ending with Brian Little scoring a hat-trick in the replay to take us through to Wembley.

Another match with Queens Park Rangers which merits a mention was the game when Everton clinched their championship win in the 1984-85 season. It was the significance of it more than the football which makes it for me. Goodison Park was full to overflowing on the Mayday holiday and all eyes were on us as we'd led the race for so long and all we needed was a win to clinch the League trophy. Goals from Derek Mountfield and Graeme Sharp took us there and that afternoon I've never felt happier. It was like a big party as we ran around Goodison to celebrate one of the finest days in the club's history.

My two other matches to remember are both finals. First the FA Cup Final against Watford and then the European Cup Winners Cup Final against Rapid Vienna in Rotterdam. As I've mentioned before against Watford we felt supremely confident we were going to win. Defeat never entered our heads and because of that the nerves and tension never affected us. It meant we were all able to enjoy the day and savour our triumph which is rare for a final. More often than not you are tied up with anxiety inside and by the time you know it the game has past by.

Winning against Watford at Wembley was a match I'll treasure for ever and I'll not forget the goal I scored either. It meant along with Norman Whiteside and the old West Bromwich Albion gladiator Jeff Astle, I'd joined an exclusive band as the only players ever to score in both an FA Cup Final and a League or Milk Cup Final at Wembley. Not many people know that!

The European final in Rotterdam was again a landmark for both Andy Gray and Everton. Because it was the club's first European triumph it was an extra pleasure, and to us all winning a major competition like that meant so much. We had proved we were just as good as Liverpool, the old enemy, and my one big regret is the European ban on clubs after the Brussels riot robbed Everton of the chance to strengthen their hold on the continent.

So there are six matches to remember, but what about the men? I've been lucky I suppose in my career to play with and against some great players.

One of my biggest heroes has been Kenny Dalglish. To me he stands for everything good in football; if you wanted the perfect team you would have eleven Kenny Dalglishs. His attitude, the way he's looked after himself and how he thinks and cares about the game is unbelievable, and I count myself lucky to have played alongside such a man in a Scotland jersey. He was a super person to play with because he always seemed to be yards and a hundred ideas ahead of everyone else. You'd be thinking of something, but Kenny would have thought of it three or four minutes before. He had a unique talent. When he replaced Kevin Keegan at Anfield many thought it was a job no one could handle but I reckoned Kenny was perhaps the only man who could have done it. You ask anyone on Merseyside now about the merits of Keegan and Dalglish and Kenny will come out tops. An even harder job than replacing Keegan came Kenny's way when he took over the manager's chair from Joe Fagan. Once again Kenny has shown great determination and skill in the way he's tackled his new role. He has the intelligence and the experience to know how to control a team and when the time comes he'll do whatever is necessary to keep Liverpool on top, even if it means selling or replacing some of the men he's played alongside. Kenny, of course, has one hell of a record to follow at Anfield but I think he has the qualities to become one of the finest and most successful managers in the game and I'm convinced the Liverpool tradition could not be in safer hands.

As a striker you tend to look to your own, and my real football hero is Denis Law. As a kid in Glasgow Denis was the King of Scotland, the soccer God who could do no wrong. I remember seeing him score a goal for Scotland against England at Hampden Park one year. Gordon Banks was in goal and as the ball came in from a corner Denis met it at the near post. He was about six feet off the ground and on his bad side I might add, but his head sort of whiplashed and the ball flew into the net. It was just unbelievable and I remember hoping one day I'd be able to head a ball like that. He was every boy's hero, of course, what with his blond hair and swashbuckling style. Also he scored goals and was at the glamour club of Manchester United. I first met Denis when I was playing for Aston Villa. He was working for BBC Radio then and I surprised him by asking for his autograph. "Who's it for?" he said. "For me," I sheepishly replied. I'd always vowed I would get his autograph one day and while I was there I got one for my brother Duncan as well.

Of the players I've played against there's never been a centre half who's really worried me. Roy McFarland and Colin Todd, when they were together at Derby County, were about the best I ever came across. McFarland was a hard but fair player who was equally at home either in the air or on the ground. Todd, meanwhile, was a wonderfully gifted defender whose ballwork was spotless, and you knew it would take something special to beat those two. Dave Watson, the old England centre half, was a player I never looked forward to playing against. He was a hard man to beat and we had some great duels over the seasons. One centre half who suprised me was Joe Gallagher when he played for Birmingham City. We came up against each other in a Villa v Birmingham derby game when I hadn't been in England very long. Big Joe whacked me twice when the ball was nowhere near us. The first time he thumped me and knocked me over in the box after the ball had gone and I was taken completely by surprise. It was the first time anyone had ever done that, and a few minutes later the same thing happened again. I suppose because I was a new boy to England Joe thought he could scare me off. I'm sure I got my own back and after that not many centre halves tried any dirty tricks.

If I could field the Andy Gray eleven I would look to men I've played alongside and some of the names might well surprise you. In goal John Burridge, a man whose career reads like a train timetable: Workington, Blackpool, Aston Villa, Southend United, Crystal Palace, Queens Park Rangers, Wolves and Sheffield United are the clubs who've benefited from Budgie's brilliance. I choose Budgie for several reasons. His goalkeeping ability is vastly underrated, but to me a character like him is worth at least twelve points a season. We've laughed at him already with some of his escapades at Villa and Wolves but I've never known a man to inject so much laughter and fun into a dressing room. On the field he's certainly no slouch either. In Wolves' promotion season it was Budgie who made the most outstanding contribution. In forty-two League matches he kept twelve clean sheets. If he was two inches taller John Burridge would have been an England keeper. You can't fault him for effort and determination and I can't think of a man I'd rather be with in a crisis. I reckon Neville Southall of Everton is the best keeper I've ever come across. Big Nev for me ranks above Shilton, Jennings, Clemence and all the other big names but for an all-round performer my vote would go to John Burridge.

At right back I'd play John Gidman, a player who's had a similar career to me with injuries hitting him hard. If not for injury Giddy would have been England's right back for years, but sadly his international career has been restricted to just one appearance against Luxembourg at Wembley in 1977. Giddy though is a fine all-round defender. He can attack with the speed and accuracy of a winger and you'll not find many more reliable defenders either. Going back to our Villa days it was often said of Giddy that he could not defend too well. He was labelled as too much of an attacking player and many thought him better going forward than tackling at the back. This used to upset John and in particular on a Friday night he was often ribbed on the local radio. A chap called Tony Butler, "the mouth of Birmingham," whose catch phrase "On Yer Bike" used to echo round the city, built his reputation on having a go at people. Tony pulled no punches on his show and I often tuned in on a Friday night to have a laugh at some of his predictions and warnings. He often used to pick on Giddy and would take great delight in saying for instance that Manchester United's England winger, Gordon Hill, was going to take John to the cleaners in the match the next day. Now that upset Giddy and, if anything, made him more determined to play well. Looking back I can't think of many players who got the better of him. I would also pick John for his fighting spirit. Not many players have fought back so well from the sort of injuries he's had over the years and managed to maintain a place at the top. We are good friends, of course, because at Villa I stayed with him for some time and we both had that battle with Ron Saunders. Our friendship is so strong that the one consolation of Everton losing at Wembley to Manchester United in the 1985

FA Cup Final was that Giddy got his winners' medal. I was disappointed for Everton but could not have been more pleased for John Gidman.

At left back I'd play another old Villa colleague, John Robson. Here again was a richly talented player who never achieved the recognition he deserved, and like Giddy and Budgie I would pick him not only for his skills on the field but for the qualities he's shown off the field. John's career and his life were devastated when doctors diagnosed multiple sclerosis. At the time all the Villa players were stunned. It was a disease we'd read and heard about but couldn't believe it could hit someone so fit and young as John Robson. He'd been feeling unwell for some time and at first we all though it was just one of those things. Then overnight we learnt the worst, but the way John coped with that crisis was magnificent. He always had a smile and a word for everyone and for me he's one of the most unluckiest men I've ever met. I can remember watching Robbo play in a testimonial match Villa had arranged for him and thinking to myself what a quality player he was. John was one of football's unsung heroes. He never sought the headlines and I'm sure many people have forgotten or perhaps don't realise he was a member of Brian Clough's conquering Derby County team before he arrived at Villa. Robbo was a true professional. He liked a drink on a Saturday night after the game but to this day I've not come across many better defenders. His tackling was strong and fair, his distribution was faultless and you could not wish to meet a nicer man.

The back four would be completed by two central defenders Chris Nicholl and Kevin Ratcliffe, two skippers I've had the pleasure of playing under. Chris was a great help when I arrived at Villa Park as a fresh faced nineteen-year-old. He was a great influence on me and the rest of the Villa side and was a natural leader. On the field Chris wasn't a skipper to shout and bawl at people, he led more by example. He had the great gift of knowing exactly how to treat different players, that's why I think he'd make a great manager. Chris knew exactly which player had to be shouted at and driven hard in training or in a game and which player needed a gentler approach. He was a terrific competitor who clearly did not know the meaning of the word fear. I always felt sorry for his wife Jane, as Chris took a fair old hammering over the years. To illustrate his determination Chris even broke his nose in a practice match once. You only have to look at the clubs he's been with and all have either won promotion or prospered. I think letting Chris leave Villa Park was one of the worst decisions Ron Saunders has ever made as a manager, and I reckon he must have regretted it privately. Chris went on to lead Southampton with distinction. Again he is a true professional. I reckon he would have made a good England centre half but finished up, of course, winning over fifty caps for Northern Ireland. That highlights how daft the international scene can be because old Chris is as English as the Queen. I'd make him captain of the Andy Gray eleven, although alongside him would be another great leader in Kevin Ratcliffe, my skipper at Everton.

Ratty is very similar to Chris in that he leads by example. He is one of the most capable and commanding defenders I've seen. He's matured no end in the last couple of years because when I first arrived at Goodison it was touch and go whether he played. Sometimes he was drafted in at left back and only when Mark Higgins got injured did Kevin get his chance. He responded absolutely magnificently and with Derek Mountfield forged a valuable partnership. Ratty is the fastest thing I've seen on two legs over fifty yards. Put him in a pre-season cross-country run and you could rely on him to come in last, way behind everyone else, but over short distances Kevin was unbeatable, the Carl Lewis of Goodison. He's as hard as nails as well. Some of his tackling is too much at times and he gets away with murder, he's got such an innocent looking face! Kevin must also be one of the most difficult defenders to play against. Not many strikers find a way round him and when I've seen him up against someone like Mark Hughes of Manchester United, who's one of the best around at the moment, Ratty gives them a hell of a hard time. Kevin, I think, will be Everton's captain for years to come and if he has the same influence as captain of Wales, then the men from the valleys could well become quite a force on the international front.

So, with the defence complete, on to midfield, and my first choice there would be Ken Hibbitt, a mate of mine from Wolves. Hibby is the best two-footed player I've seen over the past years in the first division; whether it's his right or his left foot he can pass and shoot equally as well; no matter if it's a five or a fifty five yard pass or a twenty yard shot Hibby is rarely off target. He's a great competitor as well, and like me loves to win. That's really what I've gone for in my team. Thorough professionals who give everything for victory. Ken, too, was unlucky to miss out on the international scene. He won an under-23 cap for England as substitute against Wales in the early seventies, but he was unfortunate in that at the time the country was blessed with a lot of talented midfield players. Had Hibby come in another five year span or another decade, I feel sure he would have been successful on the international front as well. He is everything a professional footballer should be: skilful, hard-working and loyal to his club. Wolverhampton Wanderers have had few better men than Kenny Hibbitt and any club lucky enough to get him as a coach or even a manager in future years will surely be on to a winner.

Next to Hibby in midfield I would have Peter Reid who did such a tremendous job for Everton. Like me Reidy has had a terrible time with injuries and he showed true grit and determination in coming back and making it to the top. Peter is a player you have to work with or watch closely to really appreciate. He ran away with the PFA Player of the Year award in 1984-85 and I was amazed it took Bobby Robson so long to pick him for the England team. I suspect he was surprised by just how good a player Reidy is. He tackles like a demon, his pace is deceptively fast and again he's another who hates being beaten. Peter was one of the most popular lads in the dressing room, a down-to-earth chap who deserves every single bit of success that comes his way. He's a simple player as well who never tries to complicate the game by being too clever. If things were not going well you knew you could give the ball to Reidy and he would do something with it. He is a player who has the rare quality to turn a match single-handed. He used to make us all laugh at Everton on a Monday morning. Peter, you see, enjoyed himself on a weekend when the game was over and liked a swift pint or two at Benny's in Manchester, and when he turned up for training on a Monday morning Reidy would always look a little jaded. At Goodison it was called the "Benny Syndrome". During the week Peter was perhaps the laziest player in the squad, and was quite often excused training, but nobody ever minded. You could hang your hat on him! We all knew that come a match Reidy would be out there covering every blade of grass.

Completing the midfield would be Alex Cropley, a Scottish lad I played with at Villa Park. Again Alex is a man who has suffered more than most with injuries and never really achieved as much as his talents should have let him. I can remember being at Villa when he was signed from Arsenal and my first surprise was to discover how tiny he was. There wasn't a picking on him and I couldn't believe this was the lad who went into tackles with the strength of a lion. We didn't have to wait long to see him in action mind you. In a practice five-a-side during training I had to close my eyes rather than watch Alex throwing himself into tackle after tackle and clattering people left, right and centre. I thought to myself then, no wonder this kid gets so many injuries. He was so enthusiastic, and I reckon because he was so light Alex thought he had to throw all of his weight into every challenge. Alex was talented as well. People talk about skilful players being able to open tins with their feet, but Alex Cropley could open a can of peas from fifty yards with one of the sweetest left foots I've ever seen. He was a superb long passer, could always be relied upon to get a few goals and was a ball winner par excellence. Alex was the type of player people hated to be up against, but loved to have with them, and there's no better testimony than that.

Moving up front I'd have Brian Little in the attack. He was my first partner in English football and it's fair to say he helped more than anyone to secure my reputation as a goalscorer. You could never wish to meet a more unselfish player, and he was a joy to play with. If Brian was clear through and I was there with him, he would not attempt anything too difficult to get a goal for himself. Instead, he would not hesitate to slip the ball square for me to score. I could not have asked for a better partner and he must have been instrumental in securing at least half of my goals at Villa Park. He was a quiet and unassuming lad who rarely seemed to get carried away when he scored. Once again he was a player who was never rewarded with the international acclaim he deserved. Brian's England career was restricted to one appearance as substitute against Wales at Wembley in 1975. Ridiculous really, when you consider there wasn't a more skilful attacker in the country at the time. Had he been with Liverpool, Spurs or Manchester United I've no doubt that Brian could have been as effective as Kevin Keegan. He could do incredible things with the ball and it delights me now to see a new generation of Villa players benefiting from his knowledge as youth team coach. I often wondered whether Brian had enough ambition to go anywhere in football but, since I've been back at Villa Park, I've been convinced that Brian has more to offer than being a coach. It's a shame his career ended before its time. If not for injury, Brian could have still been entertaining us all.

Alongside Brian in my team I would have Adrian Heath, Inchy or the Jap, as he was known at Goodison. He's a player with blistering pace, great ball control and now has the confidence to try things and score lots of goals. His finishing is as good as any and for a little lad he's an amazing competitor. He always used to rib me at Goodison because he would end up getting booked more than me. I could go on ranting and raving at a referee and more often than not I'd be told to shut up and go away. Poor old Inchy would come in and say something like "Bloody hell ref," and be straight in the book. I always used to kid him that referees picked on him because he was so small. Inchy, though, is another player who's come back from injury and I feel sorry for him in that he missed out on the end of Everton's championship year and must have been within days of a place in the England team when he was injured. Again, he's a man you'd want by you in the desert, and a player who could do no wrong.

My third man in the attack would by my old mate from Everton, Graeme Sharp. When I arrived at Goodison, Graeme had the reputation of scoring magnificent goals but could never get on the end of tap-ins and score from five or six yards. He needed to get more involved in the box and in Everton's championship year Graeme started to get the tap-ins. Over night his goal haul doubled, and now he is a striker capable of knocking them in from two or twenty yards. In all modesty I think Graeme learned a few things from playing alongside me. He added a little bit of steel to his game and, combined with his ever maturing talents, he is now the sort of player that defenders hate to have up against them. And if any further proof is needed, being picked for the Scotland attack is surely enough evidence that Graeme Sharp is one of the most feared and effective strikers in the first division today.

So, the Andy Gray eleven would line up with John Burridge in goal, a back four of John Gidman, skipper Chris Nicholl, Kevin Ratcliffe and John Robson, in midfield Ken Hibbitt, Peter Reid and Alex Cropley and up front Brian Little, Adrian Heath and Graeme Sharp. And as substitute . . . well why not Andy Gray? I've heard he can be relied upon to knock in a goal or two!

15 BACK FOR THE FUTURE

I visualised the summer of 1985 as a long hot drowsy one. With Everton at the top of the football tree as League champions and masters of Europe I was hoping to sit back and bask in a bit of glory. Jan, Amy and I were moving home to a pleasant little house just off the sea-front at Formby, and we had a couple of weeks holiday booked with Kenny Hibbitt and his family in a villa in Portugal, where we could swim and play tennis to our hearts'content. That was the plan anyway but I should have known whenever I dream of things like that something always goes wrong.

Nothing, of course, went according to plan. First football suffered a terrible kick in the teeth with the Brussels riot which helped to finish Everton's immediate hopes of playing in the European Cup. We moved house all right, but after only four nights put it back up for sale as my career somersaulted with the chance to rejoin Aston Villa. Even my holiday was interrupted by football chairmen and agents, as the race for my signature hotted up. And of course, there were few of those long hot drowsy days as it rained and rained. I'll never make a clairvoyant . . . that's for sure! Mind you it started all right. Our house move went according to plan and even though Everton had signed another striker in Paul Wilkinson from Grimsby Town, manager Howard Kendall had assured me of my future.

Three or four days before we moved I went to see Kendall up at Bellfield, the club's training ground. I wanted to clear my mind before switching off for the summer. With Adrian Heath recovering from injury, I wasn't sure exactly where I stood for the future with Everton having four strikers in their first team

187

squad. The manager was surprised to see me. I knew I could not demand or be given a guarantee of a first team place, but I needed some reassurance. I told Howard Kendall the last thing I wanted as I approched my thirtieth birthday was to be ditched in the reserves. Although I loved playing at Goodison and was honoured to be in the championship squad, I would rather have left than face a season in second team football. He asked me if I wanted a move, if I was unhappy or if I was dissatisfied with my contract. I told him that as long as Everton wanted me I was happy. "I think you underestimate yourself Andy, there's always a place for good players at Everton," was Howard Kendall's reassuring message.

So, we moved house on the Friday and the following Wednesday, the day before we were due to fly off on holiday to Portugal, we had an unexpected visitor – Everton manager Howard Kendall, who brought with him the strangest of house-warming presents. As soon as I saw him at the door I knew something was up, and sure enough his present was a piece of shattering news. Aston Villa had made an enquiry and wanted to buy me back. I was absolutely stunned. My future, I thought, had been sorted out and yet here was the Everton manager talking of a transfer. "What do you think Andy? Are you interested? Do you want to leave?" asked Kendall. "I don't know boss. To be honest it's more a question of what you want. Do you want me to leave? If you want me to go, I'll go. But if you want me to stay, I'll stay. You know I've been happy at Goodison," was my answer. "The problem is I've a chance of buying Gary Lineker from Leicester City and if you decide to go, I'll have to move fast to get him," said the Everton manager. "Then it's up to you," I said. Howard Kendall looked decidedly uncomfortable and he hummed and harred for a few moments. I reckon he'd made his mind up before he came and sure enough my worst fears were proved right. "Well Andy, I think whatever you decide, I'm going to go after Lineker," was the sentence that finished my Everton career.

I was surprised because, with four strikers already at the club, attack didn't seem to be a problem. And what's more I felt I'd given more to Goodison than sweat and goals. I'd formed a wonderful rapport with the supporters who, it turned out, were as upset as me at the changes. I'm a firm believer as well that the best players don't always make the best teams. It's been proved in the past, and the Everton side that won the championship was a superb blend of men. They always said that Everton were the team with no stars but we still took the championship in convincing style. I thought Howard Kendall was trying to take a leaf out of Liverpool's book by buying when on top, but in hindsight I think his decision to go for Lineker was a panic one. The lad was a quality player, no doubt about that, but I was hurt by the suddeness of it all. If Lineker arrived from Leicester there would be nothing for me at Everton. We both knew that but agreed to leave things as they were until after the summer holidays. Howard Kendall had hardly had time to drive down the road before the phone went. Surprise, surprise, it was Aston Villa manager Graham Turner.

He told me he'd been given permission by Everton to approach me and open transfer negotiations. The next day we were leaving for Portugal but by a strange quirk of fate were flying from Birmingham airport, so I agreed to meet Villa before I went. Our secret rendezvous was at an hotel near the airport and I made for a private room for talks with the Villa manager and his right-hand-man Malcolm Beard. They wanted an answer there and then. They were scared that once other clubs got to know I was available it might lead to an auction. I was very apprehensive at first about returning to Villa, after all they often say nothing is as good the second time around. On top of that I'd left before under a cloud and wasn't sure how people would react to me going back. And as I told Graham Turner I did not want to be bought for what I'd done for Villa in my first spell there.

The manager stressed he wanted me for the qualities I'd shown with Everton and not for the Villa memories. They'd lost Peter Withe to Sheffield United and needed an experienced and colourful striker to fill his place. Both Graham and Malcolm were convinced the past had been forgotten and the fans would love to have me back. Well, the reason I left Villa, Ron Saunders, was no longer there so I could believe them on that count. I was still very undecided and there was no way I was going to rush into leaving the League champions, so we decided to talk again after the holidays.

Imagine though what state of mind I was in as we took off for Portugal. It should have been a holiday, but as we soared through the skies my mind was spinning. And it was even worse a couple of days later when I strolled into a tiny shop in Portugal to buy an English newspaper. The back page carried my Goodison death sentence. "Lineker in £800,000 move to Everton . . . Gray on way out."

The writing was on the wall. Someone at Goodison had obviously marked the paper's card and if they said Gray was on the way out, then I was. I suppose even though Howard Kendall had spelled it out before I left, I thought there was still a chance Everton might not sign Lineker which would mean there was still a future for me on Merseyside. Kenny Hibbitt and I had a laugh about it when I'd got over the shock. It was just my luck to get lumbered with something like this on my holiday. I was determined though, for Jan and Amy's sake, to relax and enjoy myself and put the whole affair to the back of my mind until we got home. Lying by the pool with a drink by my side in the scorching sun I'd just about cracked it, until some surprise guests turned up. I could feel shadows cutting out the sun as I dozed and on opening my eyes found my old mate Dave Ismay and Aston Villa chairman Doug Ellis standing over me. Doug had come with a Villa contract in his bag and wasn't going to go home without my signature on it. He'd enlisted Dave's help to find me on holiday. Like Sherlock Holmes and Dr Watson, the two of them had spent hours phoning around travel agents to try to find us. I'd not left my number or address on purpose but those two had done their detective work well.

Dave, apart from being a mate, is a devoted Villa fan and a good pal of the chairman. I was flattered they'd gone to such lengths to find me though, and realised then that Villa must have wanted me badly. Doug Ellis outlined the plans Graham Turner had for Villa and how keen they were to sign me. The Villa manager was on holiday and, fearing other clubs would be in the chase before very long, the chairman had decided not to wait any longer. They need not have worried. I'd made up my mind by then that if I was leaving Everton the only club I'd join was Aston Villa. Graham Turner, the manager, had impressed me at our first meeting and I knew the chairman well from my first spell at the club. Doug Ellis, who in the early days was christened Mr Aston Villa, was a chap I'd always admired and got on with. He's had his enemies over the years, that's for sure, but Doug is one of the few chairmen who gets really involved. He'll make a point of visiting the dressing room after every match win or lose. And what's more his heart is claret and blue. After lengthy talks with him I agreed to sign a post-dated contract for Aston Villa which really gave them first option on me. The deal was this: if I got back to Everton and found they didn't want me I'd move to Villa, but just in case there was a different plan I reserved the right to change my mind and stay at Goodison. The business done Dave Ismay and Doug Ellis returned home to Birmingham, and I got to work on topping up the sun tan.

Three days later we had another caller at the villa – a Dutchman from PSV Eindhoven. I just could not believe what was happening. Phillips, the giant electronics firm who own the PSV club, had chartered their own executive jet to bring the manager and an agent to Portugal to find me. They had spent two days in immigration going through all the arrivals for the past week or so. The manager had to go home on business but left the agent, who eventually discovered the names of Gray and Hibbitt and from there tracked us down to the holiday villa. He brought with him an official letter authorising him to negotiate on behalf of the Dutch club. He also said they'd been given permission by Everton to talk to me. I found this a little disconcerting because as yet Everton had not told me anything, but seeing the chap had come so far and worked so hard to find me the least I could do was hear him out. We sat and talked even though I told him straight off that I had agreed to sign for Villa in the event of Everton letting me go. He persisted though, and his offer was a tremendous one: PSV were prepared to give me a two year contract and their offer was much more than Villa's. The difference was well into five figures. As in the past though, money was not the main thing. I felt the chance to play on the continent had come too late in my career and anyway I'd already given my word to Aston Villa. So the answer to PSV Eindhoven was thank you, but no thank you.

I was finally able to enjoy the rest of my holiday in peace and when we arrived home we stopped for a few days with Jan's parents in Birmingham. We'd hardly undone the cases before the phone was ringing and now Coventry City wanted to sign me. They too had been given permission to talk to me and manager Don Mackay made an attractive offer, similar in fact to that of Eindhoven's. I told him the same: if I was to leave Everton, I would be joining Villa. Right then I felt in limbo. I rang Goodison Park and both Howard Kendall and secretary Jim Greenwood were still on holiday and nobody could tell me what was going on. Eventually word came from Merseyside that Everton and Villa had agreed terms and it was now up to me.

So, I signed for Villa on what was a day of mixed emotions. I was overjoyed at being given the chance to return to Villa Park and pick up the old claret and blue jersey again but I was sad to leave Goodison. The twenty months there had been fantastic by anyone's standards. I would have been prepared to play out my career there. The atmosphere and spirit amongst the players was superb. Coach Colin Harvey and Howard Kendall had always looked after me, although I suppose I was a little hurt by the way the Everton manager had cast me off. That's football though, and I have to thank him for buying me from Wolves in the first place and giving me the chance to achieve so much in such a short space of time. I was overwhelmed by the number of letters I received from Everton fans after I left; all of them thanked me for my efforts and wished me well and some even got up a petition asking Howard Kendall to keep me. It was nice to feel wanted.

As I took one last look back at Everton I thought of two things. I'd proved I could walk in the footsteps of the Goodison greats. Dean . . . Lawton . . . Young . . . and now Gray. I felt I'd won my personal battle. Secondly, I was proud to be part of a team that will go down in history. Just like England fans reel off the 1966 World Cup winning side you'll not find an Evertonian who can't recite the team that brought Goodison Park it's finest European trophy: Southall, Stevens, Van den Hauwe, Ratcliffe, Mountfield, Reid, Steven, Sharp, Gray, Bracewell, Sheedy; and the rest, such as Adrian Heath, who were with us in spirit. Everton was, and still is, a great club and wherever I go I'll always be proud to say I was once part of it.

As for Aston Villa, well they too are something special. The club was my first English love and when I arrived back I can remember walking in and seeing the lion that watches over the ground from high on the main stand roof. The motto is "Prepared," and years before I'd told people . . . once a Villa supporter always a Villa supporter, and I'm not going to change my mind now.

16 FULL TIME

So the wheel has just about turned full circle. And looking back I must admit I've no complaints. I've been luckier than most with stacks of happy memories and plenty to show for my twelve seasons in soccer. When I started out as a fresh-faced seventeen-year-old at Dundee United I had all the drive and determination in the world, with ambition to match. As I've grown older I suppose the ambitions have tended to fade and nowadays I'm happy to be out there still playing the game I love. In a roundabout way I've achieved everything any footballer could ask for. So many players leave the game empty-handed with just memories to show for all the years of toil and tension. League Championship, FA Cup, League Cup and European Cup Winners Cup is a record I'm more than happy with and I've no regrets.

People will always ask if there's anything you'd do differently given another chance. To be honest I don't think I'd really change a thing. Dundee United and Jim McLean gave me a wonderful start to my career and I always look or listen for their result when the Scottish scores come through on a Saturday. Although Glasgow Rangers were my first love, I'm glad I went to Tannadice. They gave me a chance far quicker than I ever expected, and provided a firm and friendly launching pad for the rest of my soccer travels. If I had gone to a bigger club like Rangers I might well have been swallowed up amongst the rest of the young players and forced to wait for another couple of seasons before breaking through. At Dundee United I hit the jackpot with Jim McLean who took me under his wing and devoted hours of his own time in polishing me up. It would have been good to win that Scottish Cup in my first season at Tannadice, but United under Jim McLean have enjoyed some great years. They've won the Scottish League, the league cup and enjoyed a tremendous run in European competitions.

When you look back on your career, you tend to focus on the transfers as they really were the major turning points. Although I loved my time at Tannadice, I still think I was right to move to England and Aston Villa when I did. It proved the opportunity I needed to gain experience and whatever other nations may say the English first division is still the best in the world. When I arrived at Villa Park in 1975 the club, of course, had only just returned to the first division after several desperate years in the lower leagues. The first few seasons at Villa were exhilerating. It was exciting to be in a young successful side which sadly never really flourished as it should have done. We won the League Cup and scored some impressive wins and if not for crucial injuries, I reckon the Villa team of 1976 were good enough to take the championship. We were unlucky in that Liverpool were at their peak and there's no disgrace in ever losing out to the Anfield men.

When the chance came to move on to Molineux, I think even in hindsight, it was the right thing to do at the time. I know Villa went on to win the League Championship and the European Cup after I left, but in September 1979 I felt there was no future for me at the club. Apart from being the most expensive move of my career, the Wolves transfer was also the most difficult in more ways than one. First of all there was the trouble over the medical and it took a lot of hard thinking to finally decide to go. We won the League Cup in the first season, which appeared to indicate my decision had been right, and then despite the harrowing years of relegation and financial troubles I enjoyed my run with Wolves. I'm convinced that had the club been on a firmer standing at the bank and had the directors backed John Barnwell with money to build, the Wolves could have been a great side and achieved much more. Certainly when I joined the club the foundations were there for success. It started to go wrong when the quality men such as Willie Carr, Emlyn Hughes and John Richards were replaced by ordinary players. The youngsters drafted into the side did their best but were never really good enough to live with the likes of Liverpool and Manchester United. Had the club been taken over by a Robert Maxwell type figure who was anxious for success on the field rather than assets off it, I reckon Wolves could have still made a great contribution to the game rather than slowly sinking into oblivion. I hope, for their sake, they come back. Wolverhampton Wanderers is a name which means so much to football in this country and it would be sad to see a place like Molineux, which is built more of memories than bricks and mortar, disappear.

Although I enjoyed my four years there the move to Everton could not have come at a better time. I didn't want to go down to division two with the sinking Wolves ship and desperately needed a lifeboat to refloat my career. The move to Goodison could not have worked better. It provided me with a fresh challenge and a chance to win two of English football's most coveted prizes. I suppose I would have liked to stay at Everton a little longer given the chance, but there again when the Villa offer arrived, I was happy to return to Birmingham which I've always regarded as my English home city. Villa offered me the security of a three year contract and I hope I can see my days out with them.

I'm thirty now, and plan to go on for a few more years yet. A doctor once told me I would be lucky to play past thirty-four judging by the amount of injuries and operations I've had. I've always looked after myself though, and even if I'm forced to quit at thirty-four, that would still mean seventeen years as a striker in top grade football, which isn't a bad record. It'll take something special to shift me though, and like most players as long as I'm enjoying myself and coping with first division football I plan to continue as long as I'm wanted.

In the past, many players, Jimmy Greaves and George Best are two of the finest examples, have hung up their boots early and lived to regret it. I hope I can carry on for a long time yet, and to be honest the way the first division is going these days I might even make it to nearly forty. For me the standard in the first division has declined quite dramatically over the past decade. In my opinion, the really good players stick out like sore thumbs these days and the sport is badly in need of fresh talent. When I first came down to England every team had quality players in it and there were few weak sides. To win a first team place then you had to be something special, whereas nowadays I would classify a lot of first division players as nothing better than average. I don't think some realise how lucky they are. When I look round at the first division this season you see players who ten years ago wouldn't have made it further than the reserve side, or the second or third division. Don't get me wrong, they are good honest professionals who do their best, but so many lack that extra bit of flair or invention. When you consider how much money some earn there are times when I can see why footballers take so much stick. Good players, the stars who win matches and cups and trophies, as well as delighting the fans, are worth their weight in gold but I bet there are a few old pros around now who wish they could have their time over again. Why has the standard dropped? It's difficult to pinpoint the exact reason. A lot of coaches tend to concentrate on making a team unit work at the expense of individual skill and in the last ten years winning at any price has become the main motive behind football.

The marked decline in football support has obviously taken its toll as well. When I was a kid, and that's not so long ago, every lad played football and it was the only sport which mattered. In recent years other sports, such as athletics, have attracted more youngsters. However, I believe football still has an important future once we've managed to put our house in order. Soccer is still this country's top spectator sport and too many people love the game to let it be spoiled by the mindless minority. The Brussels riot and the ban from Europe did the game a great deal of damage but if any good can come out of such a tragedy then at last football has to make a determined effort to clear out the hooligans and win back the genuine support. England, and in particular Liverpool, were harshly punished for Brussels. No one can forgive the sins, but I was annoyed at the way everyone seemed to heap all the blame onto this country. The Italian fans are certainly no angels and I think the European soccer authority UEFA, together with the host country Belgium, made mistakes as far as security, tickets sales and safety went. But there's no escaping the fact, nor should we try to make excuses for the mess English football has landed itself in. Clubs will now have to make a concerted effort to win support, whereas in the past some have tended to sit back and take things for granted.

At Villa, and other inspired clubs such as Watford, real effort has been made to win back support. More than anything we need to impress the young generation. After all the seven, eight and nine year-olds of today are tomorrow's supporters and hopefully some will be players. If they can be set the right example, some of the fun and enjoyment killed by the hooligans will come back and our game can only benefit. We need the youngsters to come along with their mums and dads as happened ten years ago, but football must live up to it's responsibilities. Sponsorship and advertising provide much needed income these days, but without the supporter football will die. And so each and every club must be made to realise that their top priority is to provide safe and entertaining soccer. The European ban doesn't help but once we've overcome the immediate problems the suspension will surely be lifted. The European Cup, Cup Winners Cup and UEFA Cup without English teams are like the Olympics without Russia and America. They need us as badly as we need them.

While I'm on the soapbox I also think it's about time the Football League made some changes as well. It's wrong for us to stick by the old tried and trusted ways, and clearly not all the clubs can survive. In my opinion the third and fourth division should be regionalised and, together with the pick of the non-League teams, three new tables should be set up: one for the north, one for the south and one for the midlands. It makes sense because how much longer can some fourth division teams survive. The travelling costs alone of taking a team from Hartlepool to Hereford must be alarming. If there were three regionalised divisions, costs would be kept down and clubs would have more money to spend on providing brighter facilities and better players for their supporters. The top clubs from each division would still win promotion and if you included some non-Leaguers in the scheme it would give more clubs a chance to establish themselves. There are several strong clubs outside the League; Telford United for one made it to the fifth round of the cup against Everton last season and surely deserve better. If clubs had more to spend it would allow them to expand their youth policy as well and if we get more kids, then hopefully the standard might well improve. The youngsters, though, should be brought up in the game properly. Whether it's me getting old or just another illustration of today's society, but there seems to be a marked lack of discipline amongst our young players.

Football can take some of the blame because nowadays young men can earn vast amounts of money at a very early age. I reckon they should be made to stand on their own feet more and encouraged to work harder, as many appear to expect too much or take things for granted, and I've noticed a marked lack of respect. When I first started out, I knew or was told my place as a junior and wouldn't dare go into the first team dressing room without knocking on the door. Today, however, you get young apprentices strolling around as though they own the place, and of course they can't be told anything. Fortunately at Villa the club spends a lot of time on educating and improving its young professionals but for the sake of soccer's future it would be nice to get all teams moving in the right direction.

That's sorted football out, but what about Andy Gray? I've two ambitions left in football but sadly one of those, to play for Scotland in a World Cup, must now be confined to my dream-world. If I have one regret it's my international career. I won my first cap for Scotland at only twenty and in ten years have played just over twenty games. In ten years at the top that's not a record I'm particularly proud of – when I started out I honestly hoped of playing fifty or sixty matches for my country. To play for Scotland in a World Cup has always been my ultimate wish but after Mexico there seems little if no chance left for me to do so now. I should have really made it to either Argentina or Spain and have always envied the players who've gone, whether they've met with success or not. Being there is an achievement in itself. To go to the finals and rub shoulders with the best in the world must be marvellous, but of course there are lots of players who've missed out. George Best never made it, and it's amazing to think that even a great England player like Kevin Keegan had just twenty minutes or so play in soccer's biggest competition. After the disappointment of not making it to either Argentina or Spain I was resigned to missing Mexico. Had the World Cup come a year earlier, or my championship winning season with Everton a year later, I think I would have won a place, but I've had more than my fair share of success and can hardly complain.

My other ambition, which I desperately hope will still come true, is to win at least one more major honour with Aston Villa. My first season back there was hardly the winning return I'd anticipated and, after riding to the League title with Everton, finding yourself staring relegation in the face was very daunting. All in all, it was about one of the bleakest soccer seasons the Midlands can ever remember. With West Bromwich Albion and Birmingham City relegated to Division Two and Wolves landing in Division Four after tumbling like a stone from the first . . . the Midlands looks a real disaster area. Aston Villa has always been the football beacon in these parts and our revival would go a long way to bringing more people back onto the terraces in the Midlands. I've never endured a more desperate season as we slowly slipped into trouble and then finally hauled ourselves out of the grip of relegation. We got off to a bad start and never really recovered, although the run to the semi-final of the Milk Cup took us within shouting distance of a Wembley final.

Villa's lack of success was basically due to inexperience. Team reshuffles and transfers brought several new faces into the side and I think everyone, including Graham Turner, realised that too many changes had been made too quickly. But having avoided the drop to Division Two by just a handful of points I believe the foundations are there for a brighter future. The appointment of Ron Wylie as first team coach has brought more confidence to the team and the arrival of Steve Hunt and Andy Blair in midfield has added much needed craft and experience.

I'm afraid that 1985-86 was hardly a vintage year for Andy Gray. It was my worst season for a long time as far as goals were concerned, but one pleasing point was that I managed to play in forty matches. For me and my legs that is something of a record! The hardest fact about returning to Villa Park was jumping from a successful team to a struggling one. I've never been envious of Everton's continued success nor, indeed, of my replacement at Goodison Park, Gary Lineker whose goalscoring has been a revelation; it was just hard to come to terms with the move. Playing in a successful side is easy compared to turning out for one in trouble. When you are winning confidence makes the ball run your way . . . but when you are losing nothing ever seems to go right and for the first time in my career I can honestly admit the pressure got to me.

When Everton were chasing the tremedous treble of the League, FA Cup and European Cup Winners Cup, the season before, there was always talk of the pressure facing the players as the matches mounted up and the finals got nearer, but when you are doing well it's nothing. Winning is exhilerating and I could live with that sort of pressure all the time. Real pressure, though, is when you have to go out and win just to survive. There's nothing like the fear of relegation to make a player sweat. The last few weeks of the season were the worst I've ever experienced as all the time we were worrying about the other struggling teams and what their results were, as well as our own. If they won, Aston Villa might drop two or three points in the table, the pressure mounts further and everything begins to close in. The fans understandably get irritated by the lack of success and the tension tells on everyone from the manager down. When Villa beat Ipswich 1-0 and then Chelsea 3-1 at the end of the season, thus escaping relegation, the feeling of relief could be felt throughout the club.

In these desperate days of decline a drop to the second division can sometimes kill a club off. Look at Wolves. It doesn't seem five minutes ago that I was part of their winning League Cup team at Wembley, but this year they'll be playing alongside the likes of Halifax Town and Torquay United. I hope last season was Villa's transition period and that this year we can emerge fresh and ready to battle our way back to the top of the first division.

My one last playing ambition would be to help Villa back to Wembley for an FA Cup Final. They've won the League title and the European Cup in recent times so to add a Wembley FA Cup win to their list of achievements would be great. Believe it or not it's seventeen years now since a Midland team made it to the Cup Final and what a way to finish by taking Aston Villa on a lap of honour with that priceless silver trophy held proudly aloft.

When the time comes to give up I hope I can stay in the game somehow. It's the only thing I know and I just can't imagine a day when I get up and haven't a club to go to. I would love to put something back into the game which has given me so much pleasure. One thing's for sure, though, judging by my past record there'll be a few more lively years yet and let's hope many more Shades of Gray.

INDEX